SUBMARINE COMMAND

HMS *Swiftsure* at high speed on the surface. Name ship of a class of six nuclear-powered Fleet submarines, she was built by Vickers at Barrow and can do some 30 knots submerged. Estimated cost £37.1m.

SUBMARINE COMMAND

A Pictorial History

REGINALD LONGSTAFF

ROBERT HALE LIMITED
LONDON

© *R. Longstaff 1984*
First published in Great Britain 1984

ISBN 0 7090 1175 X

Robert Hale Limited
Clerkenwell House
Clerkenwell Green
London EC1

Photoset and printed
in Great Britain by
Redwood Burn Limited, Trowbridge, Wiltshire
Bound by WBC Bookbinders Ltd.

Contents

Acknowledgements

I gratefully acknowledge the generous help given to me over the past ten years by many of my former colleagues in the Director of Public Relations (Navy); by Michael Hill and Jim Allaway, formerly with Submarine Command at Portsmouth; by the late Tom Clarke of Vickers, Barrow-in-Furness, who started my collection of pictures from the company's archives; by Lt-Col John Wilson of the Navy Historical Branch, who helped check through the proofs; and by the present PR Manager at Vickers Mr W. Clouter, who has so kindly coped with my enquiries for pictures and information. Mr Bruce Robertson was kind enough to lend me many pictures from his collection and finally, my thanks go to the Adastral House and Naval Historical Libraries for their help and unfailing courtesy.

Metric Conversion Table

1 nautical mile = 1.853 kilometre
1 mile = 1.619 kilometre
1 yard = 0.914 metre
1 foot = 0.304 metre
1 inch = 2.540 centimetre
1 ton = 1.016 tonne
1 pound = 0.453 kilogram

To my many colleagues in the old Wireless Telegraphy Branch
who went to war in submarines and never returned,
and to the gallant men of Submarine Command.

Introduction

'I don't think it is even faintly realized, the immense impending revolution which the submarine will effect as an offensive weapon of war. They are the battleships of the future.'

This prophetic statement was made by Admiral of The Fleet Sir John Fisher in 1904. He became First Sea Lord on 21 October 1904 and until 1910, was the Royal Navy's 'Supremo' and keen advocate of the submarine as a weapon. Even he could not have foreseen huge underwater cruisers like the Polaris submarines of today, each armed with 16 missiles, which have beyond doubt been the 'Peacekeepers' of the past two decades.

Costing some £40m without their missiles and displacing 7,500 ton surfaced, they are a far cry from the tiny Holland Class submarines ordered by a reluctant Admiralty on 8 October 1900. They displaced a mere 100 ton and cost £35,000 each. Yet these tiny craft, together with the invention of the torpedo, were to be the biggest influence on maritime strategy and tactics in the history of the world's navies, and brought about dramatic changes in warship design, weapon systems and the composition of naval forces to combat them. Combining the element of surprise with an ability to operate unsupported in enemy waters, they became the weapon which in two world wars, brought Britain to the verge of defeat. During the First World War, German submarines and submarine minelayers were officially credited with having sunk 4,837 merchant ships of 11,135,000 gross ton, and in 1917 there was believed to be only 10 days supply of food left in the country. In the Second World War, Britain and her allies lost 2,775 merchant ships of 14.5m gross ton. The disparity between numbers and tonnage is due to the fact that from 1914–18 the average tonnage was only 2,300 ton, whereas from 1939–45 it was 5,200 ton.

While the tendency has continued during the past 50 years for naval activity to become more and more concentrated, above and below the sea, the numbers of merchant ships carrying the imports and exports on which Britain depends for survival continues to fall. This makes the submarine an even greater threat to her lifelines.

The campaigners who would have us disarm unilaterally might find food for thought in the articles written in the 1970s by the Commander-in-Chief of the Soviet Navy, Admiral of The Fleet Sergei Gorshkov. The series of articles which were published in the closely controlled Soviet press must reflect Politburo thinking.

The Admiral writes: 'The increasing importance of the sea demands a strong navy. Missile carrying submarines with greater survivability in a hostile environment, are an even more effective means of deterrence.'

He considers sea power to be an instrument of policy, to be employed with military power in the pursuit of stated objectives. He openly boasts that the Western Allies have lost the power and the will to defend the sea lanes of the world, and postulates the use of a strong navy in spreading Red Power and influence across the oceans of the world.

In stressing the importance of the sea, the Admiral says that Soviet scientists have calculated that the oceans of the world which cover approximately 70 per cent of the world's surface, contain some 10 m ton of gold; 4 bn ton of uranium; 270 bn ton of heavy water, and reserves of food, raw materials and power, so vast that there is no comparison with any known reserves on land. His navy of course, embraces all the support facilities including hydrographic research, and the use of a huge merchant marine which is one of the largest and most modern in the world.

Sea operations against land targets have assumed the leading role in Soviet operational doctrine, and their construction policy, with some 65 per cent of their programme devoted to submarines, is subordinated to this role.

The Russians are building two classes of monster submarines. The Oscar is a follow-on to the Delta Class and is 4,000 ton smaller than the American *Ohio* of the Trident Class, with 24 missile tubes. The other, variously called *Typhoon* or *Typhun*, is the largest submarine in the world. Built at the White Sea port of Severodvinsk near Archangel, it displaces a reputed 30,000 ton, and is armed with 20 missiles, with an estimated range of 4,000 miles. It is now at sea.

The first will have a strategic role and the second, as recommended by Gorshkov, is for long distance work – remote from Soviet bases – on the main tanker routes where Anti-Submarine Warfare (ASW) is sparse. The bigger size will give longer endurance, allow extra space for supplies and provide sustained fighting power with more weapon reloads.

In his foreword to *Jane's Fighting Ships 1980–1981*, Captain John Moore estimates that the Russians could operate more than 170 submarines simultaneously in the Atlantic, Mediterranean and Arctic, with reserves for the Indian Ocean and the Pacific. To combat these, the Allies could muster some 200 surface warships and 40 'killer' submarines – less escort and ASW vessels than Britain and her allies had in 1939 to meet the threat from 57 German submarines when war broke out. To the Soviet Union, the use of the sea is a bonus. To the USA, the UK and NATO, the use of the sea is a necessity for survival. It is against this background that Britain's decision to replace Polaris submarines with Trident-armed ones must be judged.

Robert Fulton's *Nautilus* was first taken to the French Government in 1797 for use as a submersible against the British Navy and trials began in 1800. The iron-framed hull was covered with copper sheeting and propulsion was by a hand-cranked propeller when submerged. Fulton and his crew of two, submerged to a depth of 25 ft in Le Havre harbour and covered an estimated 1,500 ft underwater. The vessel was armed with a detachable 'torpedo', or explosive charge, which could be fastened beneath the hull of an enemy ship. Rejected by the French, Fulton offered it to the British and found Prime Minister Pitt enthusiastic.

Trials were carried out off Walmer Castle and the brig *Dorothy* was blown in two by charges fixed beneath it by the crew of *Nautilus*. This prompted the scathing remark from Admiral Lord St Vincent: 'Pitt was the greatest fool that ever existed to encourage a mode of warfare which those who commanded the seas did not want, and which, if successful, would at once deprive them of it.'

Did Robert Whitehead with his torpedo influence the later successful design of the Holland Class submarine? Whitehead had travelled widely throughout Europe as an engineer improving silk-weaving machinery and in 1856 became technical director of a marine engineering company. He was approached by a retired Austrian naval captain, Giovanni de Luppis, with plans for a floating torpedo driven by a small motor and controlled by tiller lines. It was not viable but the idea led to Whitehead developing in 1866, the first automatic torpedo which could travel beneath the surface to attack the enemy. This 14-inch weapon, 11 ft 7 in long from a sharp nose to the tail, was driven by a compressed-air engine of 370 psi, with vertical fins running the full length of the body. A simple hydrostatic valve controlled depth-keeping and azimuth control was by trim tabs on a rudder, which was behind the single-bladed propeller. The torpedo had a range of about 200 yards at 6 knots. In 1868 he built a discharge tube for firing the weapon underwater by compressed air. There was a watertight door at each end for loading, after which the seaward one was opened to admit water. Two years later he improved depth-keeping with a hydrostat-pendulum device, later improved, which became 'The Secret' of the Submarine Service and remained virtually unchanged for some 40 years – a great tribute to a brilliant engineer. In 1869, trials of a 14-inch and a 16-inch torpedo were watched by Admiralty representatives and he was later invited to England to demonstrate them.

On 31 August 1870, the paddle steamer HMS *Oberon* moved out of the Medway for firing trials with Admiralty representatives on board, including Lieutenant Arthur Wilson (later Admiral of The Fleet Sir Arthur, VC) – junior member of the Admiralty Committee. On 7 October 1870, the former wooden corvette HMS *Aigle*, protected by anti-torpedo nets was attacked at a range of 136 yards, and the 67 lb guncotton warhead tore a hole 20 ft by 10 ft in her hull, 10 ft below the waterline.

The committee observed that the inventor had proved the properties of the torpedo and in April 1871, the Admiralty purchased the invention for £15,000 and £2,500 trials expenses. The agreement included the rights of manufacture, the training of RN officers in the 'secret' and that they be kept informed of any improvements in design. Production started at the Royal Laboratories, Woolwich, with the RL Mk 1 16-inch torpedo. Significant appointments took place later. Captain John Fisher was appointed to HMS *Excellent* for torpedo duties in HMS *Vernon*, on 30 October 1874. HMS *Vernon* was commissioned as a separate school on 26 April 1876. Fisher became Director of Ordnance at the Admiralty on 1 November 1886, and Wilson, Captain of HMS *Vernon* on 1 January 1889. Further developments and improvements led to the Royal Navy being the first to operate the 18-inch torpedo, which was the mainstay of the Grand Fleet during the war.

John Philip Holland said of his submarine: 'The submarine boat is a small ship modelled on the Whitehead torpedo, subject to none of its limitations, improving on all its qualities except speed, for which it substitutes incomparably greater endurance.'

By 1900 the submarine, mated to the torpedo, was a viable system. But still a reluctant Admiralty remained aloof. There were three outstanding designers, Lake and Holland from America, and the French gun expert Maxime Laubauf. Lake deserves a place of honour for although he lost the race to Holland, he proved that a submarine need not take an angle downwards when diving, but could be submerged on an even keel by destroying positive buoyancy. He fitted four hydroplanes, two forward and two aft, to maintain an even depth when submerged.

During the debate on the Naval Estimates in 1900, the First Lord, George Goschen said: 'The Admiralty are not prepared to take any steps in regard to submarines, because this is only the weapon of the weaker nation. If however, this vessel can be rendered practical, the nation that possesses it will cease to be weak, and will become really powerful. More than any other nation, we should have to fear the attacks of submarines.'

The First Lord was informed that on 11 April 1900, after extensive trials, the US Navy had purchased a Holland-type submarine. He wrote privately to Isaac Rice, whose firm monopolized the storage-battery business in America. After a trial in a Holland submarine which used his batteries for underwater propulsion, Rice founded the famous Electric Boat Company and purchased Holland's patents. In July 1900, through the courtesy of Lord Rothschild, Rice began negotiations with the Admiralty and with their blessing, approached Vickers Son and Maxim. An agreement, granting a licence to manufacture the Holland to Vickers, was signed on 27 October 1900.

Reginald Longstaff   Farnborough, Hants, March 1983

1

THE BIRTH OF THE COMMAND

When John P. Holland, an ex-Irish schoolteacher, emigrated to America in 1873, he was financed by the anti-British Fenian Society to build a 14-ft submersible. It was intended to be carried in the holds of merchant vessels and released in ports and harbours at night to attack unsuspecting British warships.

In 1888 he won a design competition sponsored by the American Government to design a submarine and in 1895, the order to build it. Named the *Plunger*, it ran into teething troubles and Holland subsequently returned the funds to the American Government, and took a gamble on building his own submarine. Launched on 18 May 1897, it was driven on the surface by a petrol engine, and by an electric motor when submerged. The American Navy purchased it on 11 April 1900, and it was commissioned on 12 October that year as the USS *Holland No. 1*. It was designed for a diving depth of 100 ft. The subsequent improved Hollands provided the design for the first British submarines.

Lord Selbourne, then the First Lord, announced the order for five Holland Class submarines during the debate on the 1901 Naval Estimates, and felt constrained to say: 'What the value of these boats may be in any future naval warfare can only be conjectured.'

The first significant appointment in the history of Submarine Command was that of Captain R. H. S. Bacon, a gifted and talented torpedo specialist, then at what is now the Royal Naval College, Greenwich. After Lord Fisher decided to build up the submarine branch and appoint a Commander with a free hand to experiment, organize and develop it, Captain Bacon applied for and was later appointed as the new arm's first Commanding Officer. He was later appointed as the first Inspecting Captain of Submarines. At Barrow, it is recorded that Captain Bacon found discrepancies in the drawings and stated that they must be wrong. He was supported in his contention by an American submarine expert, Captain F. T. Cable, who had come over from America with an experienced crew, to superintend the trials. It was not until one Holland nearly capsized during dock trials that the Admiralty agreed to modifications being made. A number of improvements were also suggested by the project leader at Vickers, Mr James McKecknie, some of which were incorporated in the later Holland Class, and resulted in the first Bacon-Vickers design for the A Class.

HMS *Hazard* commissioned as the first submarine depot ship and the first 10 volunteers arrived: Lieutenants F. D. Arnold Forster, S. Bowle-Evans and J. B. Moreton; Engineer Robert Spence; Petty Officers First Class William R. Waller, F. C. Knight, Joseph B. Rees, Ernest E. Neville, and Engine Room Artificers Third Class, William J. Robinson and William Muirhead.

The first British-built Hollands were to the same basic design as the USS *Adder*, lead ship of the improved Holland Class, for which the American Navy had placed an order for seven. 'Yard 280' emerged as *Holland No. 1* and was launched from the Vickers yard at Barrow on 2 October 1901. She cost £35,000, a price Rice had agreed to hold for five years, and this tiny vessel marked the beginning of submarine construction, design and development at the yard. In September 1982, this very submarine was raised from a watery grave off Plymouth after 70 years, and the 60 ton of water inside was allowed to drain off to prevent any stress. Immediate protection provided included washing down the outside with water jets, and the hull was moved rapidly to its berth where additional precautions against deterioration or crumbling were undertaken. *Holland No. 1* was refurbished and put on display near the Submarine Museum late in 1983.

With a crew of two officers and five men, the Hollands were just 63 ft 10 in long with a beam of 11 ft 10 in. They displaced 113 ton surfaced and 122 ton submerged. They were propelled on the surface by an Otto petrol engine of 160 hp which gave a speed of 7.5 knots. Submerged, a bank of 60 Chloride Company electric cells producing 120 volts, with a capacity of 1,840 amp-hours, drove a 70-hp electric motor to give a speed of 6 knots. On the surface her radius of action was 235 miles, and beneath the surface, 20 miles at 3 knots.

A single 18-inch bow tube with two reloads was the weapon fit. We have seen how the working drawings supplied to Vickers had some discrepancies. The major worry was the almost complete lack of communication with the Holland Company and the fact that the construction of *Holland No. 1* was ahead of that for the prototype Adder Class boat so that the drawings had in fact not then been proved. During the Holland programme, Vickers severed their connection with the American company and set up their own design staff.

These first submarines were packed full of danger and discomfort. There was no conning-tower as we know it today, only a small raised superstructure 32 in in diameter, made of 4-inch armour plate, for the use and protection of the navigator. This raised opening had small

Launch of a Holland-type submarine – possibly the Navy's first – at Barrow in 1901. The small superstructure can be clearly seen.

Nobody has yet proved whether HMS *Holland No. 5* above was being launched or lifted from the water when this picture was taken in 1902. *No. 5* was the last of the founder submarines of Submarine Command.

Top right is *Holland No. 3* on the surface in Portsmouth Harbour with HMS *Victory* in the background.

glazed ports in it and in the original design – without a periscope – the
boat was 'porpoised' up and down every few hundred yards so that the
navigator could take a 'bearing'. The glazed ports provided limited
illumination when running on the surface, but in the main, the crew
had to rely on electric torches and a few dim electric-light bulbs when
running submerged. Being on the bridge meant standing in that
small opening just a few feet above sea level, clinging to a handrail. In a
roughish sea the hatch had to be slammed shut continually to stop
water flooding into the submarine, and to prevent the danger of
creating deadly chlorine gas from a mixture of sea-water and
unshielded batteries. The electrical equipment sparked frequently,
and with the petrol engine giving off toxic fumes in abundance and the
low flash point of raw petrol, there was the ever present risk of an
explosion to add to the general discomfort.

There were no cooking, washing, heating or accommodation
facilities, and on passage the crew just 'camped out' where they could.
The magnetic compass was mounted outside the hull where it was free

of magnetic interference, and was viewed through an unreliable tube fitted with mirrors. It could just be seen when dived. There was a pump to control the internal trimming tanks when restoring surface trim and an air compressor to charge up the air bottles for firing the torpedoes or blowing the main ballast tanks. Both were driven off the main motor. Trim was adjusted by pumping water fore and aft, and there was an 'automatic' correction for fuel burnt. The boat was dived by operation of the single horizontal 'hydroplane' aft. The single pressure hull and framing was designed to withstand a dive to 100 ft but in practice the limit was 50 ft except in an emergency. The interior smelt strongly of petrol vapour, damp, sweat and stale air and in the early days they carried white mice to warn of danger. If a mouse turned its toes up, then it was time to do something about getting fresh air into the boat!

Captain Bacon (later Admiral Sir Reginald, KCB DSO), can be said to have invented the periscope. He first thought of the idea and it was designed by Howard Grub, head of a Dublin optical company. As fitted, it could not be extended and had to be in one of two positions. It was raised vertically to its full height of 10 ft by means of a ball and socket joint, or stowed horizontally when not in use. Objects viewed ahead were seen in their proper perspective, but those viewed astern were upside down! Nevertheless, Bacon's periscope was adapted by the US Navy.

Small wonder then that these early submariners, often dressed more like fishermen than the crew of a Royal Navy warship, were viewed with suspicion by their smarter contemporaries on board surface warships. They became known with some disdain as 'The Trade', a nickname later cherished and built into a reputation for professional expertise and contempt for danger – a tradition which has lasted to this day.

The limitations of the Holland Class were realized by the Admiralty long before they went to sea. Much of the Hollands' development work had been done in sheltered waters and the submarines had small buoyancy, a low free-draining superstructure and no bridge. They were only suited for operations in calm waters but building them enabled the Admiralty and Vickers to gain valuable early experience in submarine construction. Eventually, when all five Hollands were at Portsmouth, a series of protracted trials and experiments began in the possible uses to which these 'night torpedo boats' could be put. Defects and breakdowns were overcome and these tiny craft became amazingly efficient. They never lost a man and were easily controlled underwater. From *Holland No. 2* onwards, the submarines were of slightly larger displacement and were fitted with more efficient engines. They took part in the Fleet exercises during the summer of 1904 with five whole days of attacks on the Fleet. Each submarine operated two crews to get maximum benefit from the exercise, and at the end they claimed to have torpedoed two battleships despite protection from nets, patrolling torpedo boats and pinnaces.

On 20 April 1904 Admiral Fisher, who was then C-in-C Portsmouth, wrote in a letter: 'Here at Portsmouth, the battleship *Empress of India* engaged in manoeuvres and knowing the submarines were about, was nine miles beyond the Nab Light. So self-confident are they that the Captain is seeing defaulters and suddenly, a Whitehead torpedo misses their stern by a few feet. . . .'

He went on to say that this was done by a young lieutenant probably out on his own for the first time in a small submarine using a periscope and with an inexperienced crew.

In a statement made to the House when introducing the 1904–5 Estimates, the First Lord said: 'Captain Bacon and Messrs Vickers Son and Maxim together were authorized to supervise the construction of the submarine and to improve the type. So ably did they deal with this matter that even before the first Holland submarine was launched they had already evolved and laid down what is known as the A Type. After the A Class there has been a still further development to the B Class. We now have thirteen of these boats on our Navy List, exclusive of the five original Holland pattern. Also there are ten more in an advanced state of construction. These boats have been constantly at work during the past two years and have proved themselves very reliable.' He then went on, however, to take the typically short-sighted Admiralty view when he said their role would be supplementary to that of the surface torpedo craft and they might classify a submarine as a torpedo boat of moderate speed and very considerable radius of action. 'There is one other immediate and very important function of the submarine and that is the defence of our ports, harbours and coasts. These vessels will not only defend the ports but link up the defences and the possession of a sufficient number of them would greatly reduce the anxiety of any Admiral entrusted with the defence of our coasts.'

The follow-on classes were not to be so lucky as the Hollands and some disastrous accidents marred progress during the years leading up to the 1914–18 war. *A1* was laid down in 1902 and completed in 1903. While still at Barrow there was an explosion on board due to a pocket of hydrogen forming. Fortunately it did not wreck the entire hull but it did serve as a warning to all future submariners of the need for extreme care.

In the photograph of *A1* the various improvements can be seen. Like the Bs and Cs which followed, she was intended for coastal defence and the three classes became known as 'Fisher's Toys'. A fairly high conning-tower had been added with an open bridge built round it and three ventilating pipes were fitted, together with the periscope. Some 40 ft longer than the Hollands with a slightly larger beam, the As carried a crew of 11, and were driven on the surface by a more powerful 16-cylinder petrol engine of 450 hp to give a surface speed of 11.5 knots. An 80-hp electric motor gave a submerged speed of 6 knots. During construction of *A1* it was decided that a larger torpedo capability was required and from *A2* onwards, two 18-inch bow tubes were fitted side by side, and two reloads were carried.

The *A1* laid down in 1902 was the first submarine of all-British design. It had a surface range of 500 miles, a diving depth of 100 ft and a submerged endurance of 20 miles at 6 knots. She was the first of a class of 13, all completed at Barrow from 1903–5. The experimental *A13* was fitted with a heavy-oil engine and completed in 1908. So many design changes were made that the class may be thought of as *A1; A2–4; A5–12;* and *A13*. Still limited by endurance and speed, they were only a marginal advance on the Hollands, were not good sea boats, had cramped and very basic 'accommodation' and poor underwater performance. The *A1* was to have a tragic end.

Hoping for a spectacular success, Captain Bacon sent the *A1* to ambush the cruiser HMS *Juno* and on the last day of the exercises, 18 March 1904, the target was sighted just off the area where the Nab Tower now stands. Manoeuvring into position for an attack, Lieutenant Mansergh failed to see the liner *Berwick Castle*, bound for Southampton, through his periscope. The liner ploughed across the submarine, holed the conning-tower, and sent her to the bottom with all hands. This was the first British submarine disaster. Following this loss, all submarines were fitted with a second watertight hatch at the base of the conning-tower, so that even if holed, water was prevented from entering the pressure hull and flooding the boat. Salvaged and refitted, *A1* became the submarine in which one of Britain's most famous submariners, Lieutenant Max Kennedy Horton, learnt the art of submarine warfare.

Another accident occurred when Lieutenant Martin Nasmith in *A4* was experimenting in underwater signalling with the tip of the boat's ventilating tube sticking up out of the water, and with a torpedo boat circling at intervals. A steamer passed too close and sea-water flooded down the tube sending the boat plunging 90 ft to the bottom. Despite the clouds of chlorine gas which quickly formed, the First Lieutenant

The first A Class (1903) received a small conning-tower and an elementary bridge. Awnings could be lashed round it to protect the crew. *A3* above, was sunk in collision off the Isle of Wight in 1912.

– Lieutenant P. Herbert – found the controls, blew the tanks and brought *A4* to the surface. In *A5*, an electrical spark ignited petrol vapour and the resulting explosion killed six of the crew and injured others.

These accidents did not stop this youngest branch of the Royal Navy pressing ahead with determination and enthusiasm, even though accidents happened when everything seemed to be going smoothly. On 8 June 1905, *A8* was operating off Plymouth breakwater and following astern of the depot ship at about 10 knots. She suddenly disappeared and only four of her crew were saved.

The official inquiry could only find that the submarine foundered through developing a considerable inclination downwards while moving through the water at 10 knots.

Five further A boats were built, followed by eleven B Class – the first British submarines to have a fore hydroplane, and another attempt to improve performance. These had a length of 142 ft, a beam of 13.5 ft and displaced 313 ton submerged. Still with a single three-bladed screw, a more powerful 600-hp petrol engine pushed up the surface speed to 12–13 knots with a range of 1,300 miles. Underwater endurance was only 22 miles at 6 knots. The Bs, built from 1903–6 were also the first British submarines fitted with a deck casing, to give a more secure foothold when running in a seaway.

These were followed by an unprecedented 38 C Class – the first British submarines to have twin periscopes, among other major advances. The bigger one was a search periscope for general use and the second was a slimmer attack periscope, designed to minimize surface disturbance or 'feather' when raised and so allow the submarine to approach her target undetected. The Cs had a slightly greater measurement overall at 143 ft. Like the Bs, they were armed with twin side-by-side 18-inch torpedo tubes in the bows. A major step forward in the design of *C12–16* was the fitting of 'air traps' or 'air locks' for the crew of 16. The four enclosed spaces contained 16 diving helmets, and the escape route was through the torpedo hatch. *C1* was the first British submarine to carry a 10-ft Berthon boat. These improvements were fitted retrospectively into all the Bs and Cs.

It is worth mentioning here that Dunbar-Nasmith, later to achieve fame and win the VC in *E11* and a former Chief Instructor in underwater tactics at Fort Blockhouse, is credited with designing the retractable periscope and the range/distance finder used during attacks.

Still there were critics, often from the most unlikely places. On 21 October 1904, Captain Edgar Lees took over as Inspecting Captain of

The *A5* (below), completed by Vickers in 1904, remained in service through 1914–16 and was finally dismantled in 1920. *A7* foundered off Plymouth in 1914 but the remainder were sold or scrapped between 1919 and 1920.

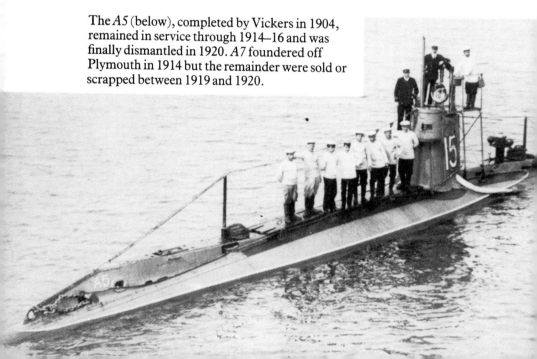

Submarines and he said during this period of major building activity: 'The British Navy has never wanted submarine boats, but a share in their evolution has been of late, forced upon us by other nations.' Lord Charles Beresford said in 1907: 'The submarine is always in a fog. They are merely a defensive weapon and therefore unsuitable for use in an offensive Fleet like the British.'

The Bs and Cs were, however, becoming well established and went on cruises, and in the *Daily Telegraph* of 8 July 1908, a reporter wrote: 'In the morning, the flotilla of 17 submarines put into Granton Harbour from Dover. The voyage was a notable performance and marks the successful development of the policy of maintaining sea-going submarine flotillas. It was accomplished in the remarkably short time of 40 hours and is stated to be the longest non-stop run ever made by a flotilla of submarine boats.' It is worth recording that *C17–20, 33* and *34* were built in Chatham Dockyard, and were the first to be built outside the Vickers yard at Barrow.

A B Class submarine fitting out in the Devonshire Dock of the Vickers' Barrow works.

It was, however, the *D1* that revolutionized submarine construction and later opened the eyes of everyone at the Admiralty to the full potential of this weapon system. She was the first British submarine with twin screws and the first to be fitted with diesel engines for surface work. Although a Vickers heavy-oil engine had been fitted in *A13* it was too heavy and cumbersome, and it was the German-invented diesel which finally did away with the danger from petrol fumes. This engine, though smaller, produced more power and allowed a bigger capacity electric battery to be installed for underwater work. The radius of action was increased to 2,500 miles and the 1,200-hp engine drove *D1* at 14.5 knots on the surface. Submerged she was capable of short bursts of 10 knots from her 550-hp electric motor.

The D Class was approved by the Admiralty in 1906 and was designed to overcome the earlier limitations of the A, B, and C Classes. The initial design work was carried out by the Admiralty for the first time on a submarine project. Eight were built between 1907 and 1912, six at Barrow and two at Chatham. They were appreciably larger than the Cs at 162 ft long with an overall beam of 20.5 ft. They displaced 495 ton surfaced and 620 ton submerged.

Major improvements included the fitting of ballast tanks outside the hull – she was the first of the Admiralty saddle-tank designs – to give more space inside the hull for the crew of 25. She was the first British submarine to be fitted with three 18-inch torpedo tubes, two bow and one stern. The bow tubes were fitted one above the other which allowed the bows to be redesigned to give a finer entry. *D1* was also the first to be fitted with a wireless transmitter and a receiver. The aerial was fitted to a mast which had to be lowered before diving, with the aerial stowed away along the side of the vessel. Experiments proved the

B1 1905 – sold in 1922.

important facts that a message could not be transmitted unless the tip of the mast projected above the surface and that signals could not be received when submerged. Prior to this submarines had only been fitted with receiving sets but even afterwards and during the war – when out of wireless range – homing pigeons were often used.

It is recorded in 1915 that when the *E6* was operating off Terschelling, Heligoland Bight, with important news to communicate, four pigeons were flown off at 04.00 with identical messages. They had to fly some 140 miles to their traps where the messages would be recovered by their owners. The message was then taken to the nearest Post Office where it was telegraphed to the Admiralty and decoded, before transmission to HMS *Maidstone* at Harwich, and again decoded. The message was received in the *Maidstone* at 15.30 – a total elapsed time of 11.5 hours. This illustrates some of the problems caused by poor communications.

A report in the *Western Daily Mercury* of 18 May 1908, when *D1* was completed, suggests that both the Admiralty and Vickers had imposed a maximum security operation. After saying that the Admiralty had

B10 completed in 1906 but bombed in a dock at Venice in 1916.

C24 which survived the war and was sold in 1921 as a result of the disposal of obsolete submarines which had started after the war. The improvements over the As and Bs can be seen clearly.

just designed a new submarine 'of which nobody knows anything', the journalist surmises that it might be the first of a new group ordered in the 1907–8 Naval Estimates and goes on: 'Immediately on taking to the water, the mysterious submarine was hurriedly towed to a wharf, barricaded on land and rendered invisible from the sea by a huge pontoon. Here she will be darkly and furtively brought to completion.'

The first Commanding Officer of *D1* was Lieutenant-Commander Little (later Admiral Sir Charles) who had earlier, in 1904, earned a place in the history of Submarine Command when ordered to take over Fort Blockhouse as Submarine Command's first shore base. This ancient fort at the western side of the entrance to Portsmouth Harbour was a fine choice. It was close enough to the dockyard amenities, but being on the opposite side of the water, could remain a separate entity. There was sufficient water in Haslar Creek for submarines to operate at all tides, and sufficient land on the peninsula for recreation. There was no ceremony. Little happened to be Duty Officer in the depot ship HMS *Hazard* and was instructed to mount a naval guard in the fort. After exchanging formalities with some Army Engineers, he returned to his duties on board.

Captain Lees had been relieved as Inspecting Captain of Submarines on 12 November 1906 by Commander S. S. Hall (Captain 31 December 1907) and the naval manoeuvres of 1910 were the first in which a submarine was used for anything but coastal defence. Admiral Sir Edmund Poë, C-in-C Mediterranean, had brought almost the entire fleet with him to join the Atlantic Fleet under Prince Louis of Battenberg. The combined fleets with their 15 battleships were Blue Fleet. Opposing them was the Red Fleet under Admiral Sir William May, C-in-C Home Fleet and his forces included the submarine *D1*, now commanded by Lieutenant-Commander N. F. Laurence (later Rear-Admiral (S) and Admiral Sir Noel. In spite of trouble with one engine, *D1* made her own way from Portsmouth to the Blue Fleet bases on the south-west coast of Scotland. There she operated unseen for three days, 500 miles from her base, until she torpedoed two Blue Fleet cruisers as they left the shelter of Colonsay.

In February 1911, as if to make the point yet again that British submarines could operate overseas on their own, *C36* (Lt Herbert), *C37* (Lt Fenner) and *C38* (Lt Codrington) steamed from England to Gibraltar under their own power. They were on their way to Hong Kong, 10,000 miles away, to join the China Squadron. Although escorted by the sloop HMS *Rosario*, these tiny craft had to cross the Indian Ocean before arriving safely.

Captain R. J. B. Keyes, MVO, later to become the first Commodore

(S), and Admiral of The Fleet Sir Roger Keyes Bt, GCB KCVO CMG DSO LLD MP, took over as Inspecting Captain of Submarines on 14 November 1910. He appointed a committee to help him of six officers, all of whom later distinguished themselves. They were Commanders P. Addison (later Director of Dockyards), C. Little and Engineer-Commander Skelton (later Engineer-in-Chief, Royal Navy); and Lieutenant-Commanders Laurence, Nasmith (later Admiral Sir Martin Dunbar-Nasmith) and Craven (later Sir Charles and Managing Director, Vickers). With such men to advise him, it was small wonder that the British Submarine Service set standards which have seldom been equalled anywhere in the world.

The post of Inspecting Captain of Submarines was unique in the annals of naval commands. Headquarters were at HMS *Dolphin*, Fort Blockhouse, Portsmouth. The Captain also had an office at The Admiralty. HMS *Bonaventure* (sea-going depot ship) and *Antelope* (tender) were also at Portsmouth. HMS *Thames* (sea-going depot ship) and *Sharpshooter* (tender) were at Harwich. HMS *Vulcan* (sea-going depot ship) and *Hebe* (tender), at Dundee. HMS *Forth* (sea-going depot ship) was at Devonport. HMS *Maidstone*, especially designed to 'mother' 12 D Class, and the *Alecto* and *Adamant* to 'mother' 3 D Class each, were being built. HMS *Lurcher* (flag) under the command of Commander Wilfred Tomkinson and *Firedrake*, were the two attached destroyers.

The Ds were the first submarines to operate successfully 500 miles from base.

D4 with the gun (above) can be compared to the earlier *D2* without a gun (below). This latter submarine was reported lost in the North Sea during 1914.

The committee also formed a tactical advisory body for dealing with material and personnel. Although the D Class had better sea-keeping qualities with greater longitudinal stability than previous classes, the committee found that the new E Class was not the last word in submarine construction. After inspections abroad, they pointed out that the Es could not be driven on the surface at a speed of 15 knots without the danger of diving suddenly, whereas the French and Italian designs could be driven at even higher speeds on the surface without any danger. Keyes has written in his memoirs how he considered it vital to shake off the 'blinding monopoly' of Vickers in order to widen the field of production, introduce competition and be in a position to build any number or type of submarine that might be required.

The Admiralty were not anxious to improve the design of periscopes either and it was felt that the cost of the best ones, at some £300 each, were luxuries they could not afford. Keyes fought this short-sighted viewpoint and said that it was ridiculous to impair the military value of a submarine costing £100,000, for want of an 'eye' costing £300. Eventually, he was given permission to select the best Italian, German and French designs, and have them built under licence in Britain, where they were further improved mechanically and optically.

On 31 March 1911, the Admiralty gave two years notice of their intention to terminate the Vickers monopoly and this left the way clear for the committee to go abroad for experimental design. Sir Philip Watts, then Director of Naval Construction, provided three designs, the French, Italian and an improved E. In February 1912, the committee also recommended the building of two types of submarines. One was an overseas type of about 1,000 ton with much-improved living accommodation, sufficient speed to operate with the Fleet and capable of extended operations in all weathers. This was the G Class. The second type was the F Class, a coastal submarine of some 350 ton.

In 1913, Messrs Scott built the S Class to an Italian Laurenti design but these proved unsuitable for North Sea operations and were eventually sold to the Italians in 1916. Armstrong built the W Class to the French Laubauf design but these too proved unsuitable and their conning-towers were too low. They were later sold to Italy. The V Class built by Vickers was of a higher displacement and proved satisfactory but for the fact that it could only average 14 knots on the surface.

Next came the *Nautilus* and the *Swordfish* – the latter being the first British steam-driven submarine, designed to do 18 knots on the surface with a radius of action estimated at 3,000 miles. None of these designs really achieved anything and were not the major advances sought after. The Es were ordered up to No. 18 in the 1913–14 Estimates.

Following a discussion in December 1913 on the potential U-boat threat, the G Class type of overseas patrol submarine (above) was designed to counter the threat. Part double-hulled and estimated to cost £125,000 each, they were propelled on the surface by the Vickers diesels as fitted in the E type with two 8-cylinder units developing 1,600 bhp to give a surface speed of 14 knots. Two single-armature motors each of 420 bhp, gave a submerged speed of 9 knots. Two battery tanks of 200 cells gave a submerged endurance of 95 miles at 3 knots.

The armament was changed to two 18-inch bow and one 21-inch stern tubes, with two 18-inch beam tubes. This design marked the introduction of the more powerful 21-inch torpedo into operational service as although fitted in the experimental *Swordfish* ordered from Scotts a year earlier, this submarine was launched after *G1*. A 3-inch gun which could be used for anti-aircraft work as well, was fitted forward of the bridge. The designed diving depth was given as 200 ft and one of the class did reach 170 ft when attacked by British destroyers – by mistake!

G1–5 were ordered from Chatham Dockyard in June 1914; *G6–7* from Armstrong Whitworth; *G8–13* from Vickers; and *G14* from Scotts on the Clyde. *G7, 8* and *11* were lost on operations; *G9* was sunk in error by HMS *Petard* off Norway; four were scrapped after the war and the remaining six were withdrawn from service in January 1921.

Although unsuccessful, the *Swordfish* was unique in being the first submarine fitted with a mix of torpedoes. As designed, she had two tubes for the new 21-inch torpedo forward. These were said to be twice as powerful as the 18-inch, for which she had four beam tubes. Despite their failures, the Admiralty did learn a lot about submarine construction and steam propulsion from this design.

By now, however, a new and improved boat of British design had been brought forward in the E Class, a vastly improved form of the Ds, and was to bear the brunt of the war years earning immortal fame. Vickers continued their successful partnership with the Royal Navy by building all the lessons gained from their experiences with the earlier classes into the Es, which were the first submarines to be built to such high standards. They were formidable fighting machines capable of world-wide operations in all weathers, with a much-strengthened hull incorporating transverse watertight bulkheads. Like the *D4* which was the first to mount a gun, the Es were progressively fitted with a 6- or 12-pdr, a 4-inch, and in one even a 6-inch howitzer.

HM Submarine *G10*.

The V Class was an experimental Vickers design for a coastal type to meet the requirements of the 1912 Submarine Committee, with four being ordered and the first laid down in November 1912. Like the new Type 2400 they were part double-hulled with the double-hull confined to the centre portion of the submarine, and the outer hull fared into the pressure hull fore and aft. Costing £75,799 each, they were powered by Vickers-designed diesels developing 450 bhp at 450 rpm, and these were the first of the company's engines to have steel instead of cast-iron cylinder jackets. Designed speed was 13 knots with a range of 1,200 miles at full power. Electric power was supplied by a bank of 132 Exide cells to give a submerged speed of 9 knots and an endurance of 50 miles at 5 knots. Diving depth was given as 150 ft instead of the normal 100 ft of previous submarines, the extra hull strength being provided by external framing between the outer and inner hulls. Armed with two 18-inch bow tubes, two spare torpedoes were stored on the starboard side of the torpedo flat with warheads stowed separately nearby. One 12-pdr gun was fitted. The torpedo hatch was mechanically operated as in the E Class. All four were taken out of service in July 1919.

With an overall length of 258 ft 4.5 in, the *Nautilus* (later *N1*) was nearly twice the size of existing submarines and was an interesting experiment by Vickers to build a submarine with good sea-keeping qualities for extended operations in all weather conditions. Although the cost was given as £203,850, changes and improvements such as hydroplane guards meant a longer building time, and the cost figure was probably exceeded. With a designed diving depth of 200 ft. *Nautilus* was, like the Vs and Gs, driven by a three-bladed propeller and the design speed was 17 knots. Endurance was stated as 5,300 miles at 11 knots and submerged, 72 miles maximum. She was armed with two 18-inch torpedo tubes fore and aft, and four 18-inch beam tubes. A total of 16 torpedoes was carried. The *N1* did not complete until October 1917, had little operational service, and was used for instruction/training purposes. The significance of the design was the experience and confidence gained in building such a revolutionary submarine, displacing 2,026 ton submerged. This provided Vickers with valuable data for the larger submarines when they arrived off the drawing-boards later.

Another view (opposite) of a G Class submarine at the Barrow works of Messrs Vickers. The starboard bow tube opening is clearly visible.

The Es were 181 ft long with a beam of 22.5 ft, displaced 660 ton
surfaced and 800 ton submerged. Two 800-hp diesels drove twin
screws to give a surface speed of 16 knots and an 840-hp electric motor
gave them 10 knots submerged. They were armed with five 18-inch
torpedo tubes, two bow, two beam and one stern, and carried a crew of
30. There were minor variations in the class which was officially
subdivided into E1, E7 and E21 types. A total of 56 were ordered of
which six were built at Chatham Dockyard; three at Devonport
Dockyard; four by Cammell Laird and William Beardmore; and
others by Swan Hunter, Thornycroft, Fairfield, Palmer and
Armstrong Whitworth. When Vickers completed the twentieth of
those they built, it was their fifty-eighth submarine for the Royal
Navy.

As early as March 1910, the Admiralty had set up a committee to
consider anti-submarine warfare and a series of trials started in the
autumn of 1912 when Admiral Sir George Callaghan, C-in-C Home
Fleet co-operated with Commodore Keyes in exercises with
submarines off the Scillies and Southern Ireland. The capital ships
were screened by destroyers and a series of progressive trials began to
find the best anti-submarine tactics to employ. After the 1913

Launch of the *E11*, later to become the command of one of Britain's most famous First World War submariners, Lieutenant M. Dunbar-Nasmith, who won the VC for his exploits in the Sea of Marmara in 1915.

manoeuvres, Captain S. S. Hall reported: 'The general feeling is one of satisfaction with the crews and their handling of submarines, particularly the D and E Classes. The submarine service seems to be satisfied that during the short time the manoeuvres lasted, they would have accounted for 40 per cent of the large vessels involved.' After the 1914 manoeuvres, those who had earlier thought of submarines as a mere extension of defensive mining found: 'The development of the submarine, rather than reducing the necessity for defensive mining, has necessitated a revival.' The committee also concluded that as there was no means of direct attack on a submerged submarine (there were no depth charges as yet), the best means of attack was to stalk the enemy and torpedo her on the surface.

The submarine was becoming recognized as a weapon which could be used to strike blows against an enemy, far from home bases, but there were still some who found the new, ruthless type of warfare ungentlemanly. In April 1914, Vice-Admiral Sir Doveton Sturdy said: 'It is high time we put the fear of God into these young gentlemen who lie about the North Sea, attacking all and sundry without let or

The unfortunate *E20* which was completed in 1915 and later that year, was torpedoed and sunk in the Sea of Marmara by the German *UB14*.

hindrance.' On 5 June 1914, Percy Scott took the opposite view and wrote: 'Submarines and aeroplanes have revolutionized naval warfare. The submarine can deliver a deadly blow even in daylight.'

By the outbreak of the First World War, the Royal Navy was the greatest submarine power in the world with a total of 74, plus 31 more being built and 14 others ordered or projected. With the exception of three Bs at Malta and Gibraltar, and three Cs at Hong Kong they were all in home waters. Britain's major weakness was the fact that out of this total, when war was declared on 4 August 1914, she had only 18 of the D and E 'overseas' submarines – perhaps the direct result of going abroad for new designs.

The period of 'strained relations' prior to the outbreak of war saw the submarines taking up their war stations. The 8th Submarine Flotilla of D and E Classes, based on the depot ships HMS *Maidstone* and *Adamant*, was under the command of Captain A. Waistell (later Admiral Sir Arthur) and operated under the orders of the Admiralty. Attached were the destroyers HMS *Lurcher* (in which Commodore Keyes flew his Broad Pendant) and *Firedrake*. They arrived at Harwich on 31 July 1914 and were to work under the first Admiral of Patrols, Rear-Admiral John de Robeck. They at once made plans for co-operating with Commodore Tyrwhitt's force of light cruisers and destroyers based on the same port, and these plans included a reconnaissance of the Heligoland Bight immediately after war was declared. Most of the B and C Classes joined up with the surface patrol flotillas working out of Britain's principal ports, the most important being the Dover Patrol. The remainder, including the older As, were attached to harbour defence flotillas.

By 1914, torpedoes were costing some £800–£900 each and the practice ones used in exercise attacks were controlled so that they rose to the surface at the end of their run, and could be recovered. This single factor was to cause a lot of trouble during the early months of the war and led to many targets being missed.

It would be inappropriate to catalogue a list of individual actions in a book of this kind, as it has been done in great detail in many of the books listed in the bibliography. The incidents and events that are selected are those which I believe tend to highlight the development of the submarine during the intense activity of two world wars, and in the peaceful years between.

2
A CHANCY 'TRADE'

To see – but be unseen! This dictate of all submariners was fraught with danger in a period when recognition training was minimal and any conning-tower or periscope seen was presumed to be that of the enemy. The only safe action was to attack and many of Britain's submarines were on the receiving end of 'friendly' hostile action.

A brief non-technical description of how a submarine works might prove of interest to the general reader. The E Class had a small bridge capable of holding three men which was reached from the submarine casing by a short vertical ladder. Through this tiny 'deck' rose the two periscopes and the wireless aerial mast, raised or lowered by a handle. The hull was like a metal cigar with the saddle-tanks bulging outwards on either side. These were the main ballast tanks and when water was let in to fill them, they destroyed the boat's positive buoyancy and let it submerge. A vertical ladder led from the upper conning-tower hatch, through a second hatch, to the control room. Both the hatches were watertight.

These modern submarines had a thick pressure hull which was designed to withstand the sea pressure at the designed maximum diving depth but, as events proved, often stood up to far greater depths. Outside it was the thin outer hull of the main ballast tanks, which were not required to withstand sea pressure (45 lb per square inch at 100 ft). On the surface the main ballast tanks were open to the sea at the bottom but the water was kept out by air pressure, locked in by quick-acting main vents at the top. When the submarine was trimmed down ready for diving, only the conning-tower showed above water. The submarine was, in fact, riding on air.

The diving klaxon would sound; the main vents would be opened, and as the air rushed out the sea poured in. A thump on the back would send the signalman or watchkeeper diving through the open hatch at his feet, and down the vertical ladder in a controlled slide. The officer on duty would follow, clipping the upper and lower watertight hatches as he came down. These early submarines could be at their periscope depth of 30 ft in 30 seconds, moving slowly ahead on their electric motors. The diesel engines, which needed air to operate, would have been shut off as every bit of air inside the submarine had to be carefully conserved.

When properly trimmed underwater a submarine is in perfect

balance with no tendency to rise or fall, but passing through water layers of different density can make her lighter or heavier. Depth is maintained by the forward hydroplanes and the angle at which she lies in the water by the after ones. The First Lieutenant or No. 1 must see that the submarine remains steady at her depth, by the use of internal tanks within the pressure hull. He must constantly make allowances for fuel, oil, food, torpedoes or gun ammunition expended – all of which make the submarine lighter. Like a bicycle, balance is more easily maintained when moving at a 'fast' speed, but when hunted, a submarine might have to go into silent routine with electric motors stopped, and the trim then calls for expert and precise judgement.

Right forward were the bow torpedo tubes and through the watertight bulkhead just behind them, the storage space for four torpedoes in racks, two on either side. Here, in this cramped space, some of the crew ate and slept. Through the top of the pressure hull was a large watertight hatch, only opened in harbour for loading torpedoes. Below them as they slept, was the No. 1 battery of 111 cells, each weighing half a ton. The deck had to be lifted to top them up with distilled water when needed.

After this, in the direction of the stern, came the small ward-room leading directly to the control room itself, which to the layman looks like a hopeless tangle of pipes for the hydraulics, high-pressure air and the electrics. The helmsman sat at the steering-wheel and the two coxswains operated the fore and aft hydroplanes, controlled by large wheels. In front of them was the most important piece of apparatus in the boat, the depth gauge. On the starboard-side opposite was the big switchboard with its huge electric cables running aft to the electric motors. The hydraulics controlled the two periscopes, the vents for the main tanks and the high-pressure air valves for blowing the water out of the tanks when surfacing. Below the deck was No. 2 battery and the two beam torpedo tubes.

Next, towards the stern, came the diesel-engine room with its air compressor for charging the high-pressure air 'bottles' and pumps for trimming the internal tanks. Last was the motor room controlled by a torpedo-man at the control board. Right aft in the same section was the stern torpedo tube. A system of clutches allowing the diesel or electric motor to drive the propeller. When charging batteries on the surface, a diesel engine drove the electric motors as dynamos.

The early days of the war were to teach a lot of lessons. The paramount duty of the Home Fleet was to secure command of British waters to ensure the safe passage of essential supplies. That Britain was later accused of being unprepared was not due to lack of foresight, but to the never-ending change in power, range and character of naval material, which left no firm foundation on which to build a sound defence. So rapid were developments that extensive naval building programmes tended to be out of date before they were completed. It was evident that owing to the increased range, speed and power of torpedoes, Britain's main anchorages could be exposed to attack. The home defence forces included eight flotillas of submarines and the 8th (offensive) arrived at Harwich on 31 July 1914, supported by the depot ships *Adamant* and *Maidstone*. When war broke out on 4 August 1914, the flotilla comprised eight Ds and nine Es. A total of 37 Cs and 10 Bs made up five flotillas working out of the defended ports of Chatham, Dover, Humber, Tyne and the Forth. Three flotillas of the early As were assigned to harbour defence duties.

The enemy now had a fortress to the east of the North Sea with two widely separated exits from it linked by a well-protected waterway, and were secure behind coastal and base defences. They could not be brought to battle unless they chose to come and seek it. The High Seas Fleet could be kept intact while the British patrolling warships and ports could be hindered by minefields and harassed by lightning attacks from surface ships or submarines. It followed from the start that British submarines should play an offensive role in the Heligoland Bight, and later in the Baltic and the Dardanelles. War between surface warships and submarines was a new experience. British submarines had to probe into heavily defended enemy waters, patrolled by the enemy without real danger of engagement by British surface warships. The early Bight patrols were intended to provide the valuable knowledge of enemy movements in fairly shallow waters, where the enemy would be fully alerted if a submarine was seen.

At 03.00 on 5 August, Lt-Cdr Talbot in *E6* and Lt-Cdr Goodhart in *E8*, towed by HMS *Amethyst* and *Aerial*, slipped their tow off Terschelling on a reconnaissance trip and provided valuable information for the Admiralty. These were broken off on 8 August and the submarines of the 'Overseas' Flotilla covered the movement of the expeditionary force to France for seven days – their first experience of an extended patrol at sea.

It seems incredible today to believe that in wartime submarines could be moored to buoys across the English Channel. Yet this was standard practice for some weeks and it was not until after an abortive U-boat attack that a general order was issued that no submarines were to secure to the buoys in future.

Between Dover and Calais there were three sets of buoys at equal

HM Submarine *E5* which, as was normal practice in those early days, was identified by a number on the conning-tower and E4 on either side of the bows. She was lost in the North Sea in 1916.

intervals. The B and C Class submarines all worked three days at sea followed by two in harbour. They spent the first day at buoy 'a', the second at 'b' and the third at 'c'. Six submarines would be moored to the buoys waiting for an enemy-sighting report, and to conserve fuel. Three others would patrol the areas at slow speed. There was of course no anti-submarine organization in being and on 27 August Lt-Cdr A. C. M. Bennett in *B3* was moored to buoy 'a' with the patrol craft HMS *Attentive* in company. At 14.30 the *Attentive* was attacked by a U-boat but fortunately, the torpedo passed ahead of the target.

On 21 August, the German cruiser *Rostock* set out for the Dogger Bank and was sighted by *D5* (Lt-Cdr Herbert) who manoeuvred to make it a 'sitting shot' target at 600 yards and fired two torpedoes. Nothing happened! It is now known that the two torpedoes passed under the cruiser which had a draught of 17 ft, and as Admiral Sir Roger Keyes was to write later: "It was some time before we discovered that our warheads were some 40 lb heavier than the practice torpedoes with which we exercised." The result was that the torpedoes did not pick up their set depth until after a considerable distance and so ran deep under the target.

An operation planned on 28 August to intercept enemy forces at sea brought about the first major rescue by a submarine *E4* (Lt-Cdr E. W. Leir). On the first engagement of the day the German destroyer *V187* was sunk and HMS *Defender* lowered her boats to pick up survivors. Shortly afterwards a German cruiser loomed up out of the mist and the force were ordered to retire. Lt-Cdr Leir surfaced, took on board a lieutenant and nine ratings from the *Defender*; one officer and two men from the German destroyer 'as samples', and provided the rest of the Germans with the boats, food and a compass, to get them back to Heligoland.

Meanwhile the 'accounts' were being opened. On 9 August 1914, the *U15* was seen on the surface at dawn, rammed and sunk by the cruiser HMS *Birmingham*. The first sinking by a submarine was, however, by the German *U21* which torpedoed and sank the flotilla leader HMS *Pathfinder* off St Abbs Head on 5 September.

On 12 September, the legendary Max Horton in *E9* was lying on the bottom at 120 ft and about six miles SSW of Heligoland. He surfaced to periscope depth at daybreak and saw the light cruiser *Hela* – an elderly warship which had been used as the 'yacht' for the German C-in-C. He closed to 600 yards and fired two torpedoes. One hit amidships and the cruiser sank. On 6 October he completed a unique 'double' when he torpedoed and sank the German destroyer *S126* off the Ems – a feat described by Commodore (S) as 'like shooting snipe with a rifle'.

Meantime, on 22 September, the submarine had made its mark and established itself in history as a major weapon of attack not defence. The *U9*, commanded by the famous German submariner Otto Weddigen, torpedoed and sank three old cruisers, HMS *Hogue*, *Cressey* and *Aboukir*, with the loss of nearly 1,500 lives.

The cruisers were part of the Southern Force under Admiral R. H. Christian in his flagship *Euryalus* and included the 7th Cruiser Squadron of *Bacchante*, *Aboukir*, *Cressey*, and *Hogue*. Independent of the force were ten submarines of the 8th 'Overseas' Flotilla and the attached destroyer *Firedrake*. They were to safeguard the lines of communication for the Dunkirk landings and at 05.00 on 20 September, the Admiral was off the Maas lightship with the three cruisers. Bad weather prevented a destroyer-screen operating and the three cruisers were left to keep the 'Dogger Bank' patrol on their own.

Just before 06.30 on 22 September there was an explosion under the stern of *Aboukir* and 25 minutes later the cruiser turned over and sank. 'Abandon ship' was sounded but there was no steam to hoist out the boom boats and the crew took to the water. The *Hogue* closed on the survivors and was struck by two torpedoes. While her boats and those of *Cressey* were returning with some survivors, the *Cressey* was struck by two torpedoes and sank. Some 60 officers and 800 men were saved.

As a result, a General Fleet Order was issued that if a major warship was torpedoed or mined, she was to be left to her fate and other ships were to leave the danger area immediately and call on minor ships for assistance.

Nothing that had happened before so dramatically changed the concept of naval operations at sea. The 'unseen' attacks were bringing results which the strongest advocates of the new weapon had predicted earlier. The submarine was the lone wolf, the unseen enemy, able to operate with impunity in the 'front door' of the strongest naval power in the world and cause enormous damage with loss of life. It was a new factor to be reckoned with in a new warfare. The lesson should have been learned too – but was not – that the submarine could not operate with the Fleet in war conditions, because it was not only difficult to recognize a friendly submarine on the surface, but after this tragedy, every periscope sighted had to be attacked as a potential threat. Later in the war when the *U29*, commanded by Weddigen, was returning from another successful sortie off the Scilly Islands, the submarine was rammed and sunk by the battleship HMS *Dreadnought* and cut in two.

The first British submarine loss of the war was *E3* (Lt-Cdr Cholmley), which pushed too far into the western Ems in search of targets, and was cut off by destroyers and sunk by *U27*.

Admiral Prince Louis of Battenberg resigned as First Sea Lord on 28 October 1914, on grounds of his German parentage and Lord Fisher returned to the post on 31 October. He noted with regret that the submarine strength was not much better than when he left office in 1910. On 28 October, the First Lord Winston Churchill had written to the First Sea Lord: 'Please propose without delay the largest number of submarine boats to be delivered from twelve to twenty four months from the present time.

'You should assume for this purpose that you control all the sources of manufacture required for submarines, that there is no objection to the use of Vickers' drawings and that steam engines may be used to supplement oil engines. You should exert every effort of ingenuity and organisation to secure the utmost possible delivery. As soon as your proposals are ready, which should be in the next few days, they can be considered at a conference of Sea Lords.

'The Cabinet must be satisfied that the maximum output is being worked to in submarines. We may be sure that Germany is doing this. The Third Sea Lord's department must therefore act with the utmost vigour, and not to be deterred by the kind of difficulties which hamper action in time of peace.'

Lord Fisher called a conference 48 hours later which resulted in an immediate order for twenty of the overseas type to be built, and a programme of construction for American-designed boats was arranged to be carried out in Canadian shipyards. The final November War Emergency Programme specified the building of 38 Es, five of which were later fitted to carry up to 29 mines, and seven of the G Class, all to be built in the UK. Ten of the H Class were to be built, five in America and five in Canada. These were only half the tonnage of the Es but were the first British submarines to get the powerful armament of four 18-inch bow tubes. They proved so good that a further batch of the improved H21 type was ordered, mounting four 21-inch tubes.

It had become known that the U-boats had a surface speed of some 19 knots and a 13-pdr gun which outranged British submarines, and they could communicate by wireless to their bases over a distance of about 200 miles. British wireless transmitters had a range of about 50 miles and pigeons were used when outside that range.

Winston Churchill minuted: 'I await a special report on the fitting of Overseas submarines with special long distance wireless. It is indispensable that our submarines should be able to communicate with our receiving stations when operating in Heligoland Bight.' As a result, some of the Es had an internal beam torpedo tube removed to fit a special wireless cabinet.

A code for signalling between submerged submarines had been worked out by tapping with a hammer on the pressure hull and as sound carries a long way underwater, some messages had been passed over several hundred yards. Churchill wrote another minute: 'The system of sound signalling, enabling one submarine to communicate with another has been toyed with for a long time and it is now necessary to produce practical results, even if of a crude and imperfect character, which can be made rapidly effective. A report should be furnished within three days, stating what is possible and making proposals for action.'

Experiments eventually led to the Fessenden gear, virtually a metal plate which could be vibrated to give off sound waves. Its range was limited to a few miles and was not directional, so enemy U-boats could listen in as well. The listening ear was the hydrophone. Both these primitive devices were British inventions and despite their imperfections, were a great advance for the time.

Aid to Russia

Lt-Cdr C. Boyle in *D3* and Lt-Cdr A. Cochrane in *D1* had made a submarine reconnaissance of the shoal waters inside the Arum Bank and off the Sylt. This showed that it should be possible to enter the Baltic through the Kattegat and the Belts. This campaign was the first to bring the submarine into prominence and Commodore Keyes decided to send three submarines into the Baltic to bolster up Russian morale. It must be remembered that the Germans still believed that the war would be a short one and they regarded the Russians as their most formidable foes. They were therefore more immediately concerned with controlling the Baltic rather than the North Sea.

Lt-Cdr N. F. Laurence in *E1*, Lt-Cdr M. K. Horton in *E9* and Lt-Cdr M. Nasmith in *E11* sailed to force the passage. *E11* ran into trouble on 21 October 1914 when she was sighted by a seaplane and hunted incessantly. With her presence given away, she turned back for home. Laurence in *E1* entered the Baltic on 17 October and finding no targets, proceeded to Libau where he was met by a Russian liaison officer. Horton in *E9* joined Laurence on 22 October. On 30 October, other submarines joined them at Lapvik where they came under the orders of the Russian C-in-C. Eventually, there were five Es and four of the smaller C Class – which had come by sea and overland, round the North Cape to Murmansk and then by barge and train to Lapvik or Ravel – under his command.

In January 1915, Ravel suffered a severe spell of cold weather and *E9* went to sea to find out if a patrol in the icy cold waters was possible. It was found that spray rapidly froze and formed ice up to six inches thick all over the superstructure. To dive at all meant that crew members had to work continually chipping ice away from the conning-tower hatch so that it could be closed in an emergency. Trials proved that the ice formed in the main vents was more slush than solid ice and was blown out by the escaping air. When dived the warmer salt water quickly freed the submarine from its unwelcome top weight of ice. *E9* sank a collier on 5 June 1915, badly damaged the destroyer *S148* and on 2 July, off Rixhoft, badly damaged the cruiser *Prinz Adalbert*.

On 19 August *E1* badly damaged the battle-cruiser *Moltke* and on 28 August, Goodhart finished off the *Prinz Adalbert* off Linbau. In 1916 *E18* was lost in a minefield. The steady destruction of coastal shipping carrying vital war supplies and the damaging attacks on warships forced the Germans to introduce a convoy system in their home waters. *E19* (Commander Cromie) also did tremendous damage to the blockade runners carrying iron-ore to German ports.

This epic saga ended on 4 April 1918 when the Russians signed a peace treaty with the Germans. The treaty contained a clause which demanded the surrender of all the British submarines. The Senior Officer (*E19*) scuttled his own submarine, *E1* and *E8*, *C26*, *27* and *35*, rather than allow them to fall into enemy hands. Trained submariners were in short supply and most of them escaped through a wild and inhospitable country, avoiding the revolutionaries and returning to England via Murmansk. In general, the crews reported that the Russians were backward and inefficient, and under a bureaucratic regime that prevented them from exercising operational control or individual judgement.

Another major rescue at sea followed the raid on Cuxhaven by the Royal Naval Air Service (RNAS), on Christmas Day 1914. *E7* was already in position to cover the raid and she was joined by three D and six E Class submarines that sailed on the night of 23/24 December. The weather was fine and sunny when seven of the nine seaplanes took off from their parent ships *Engadine*, *Riviera* and *Empress*, from Harwich.

E11 dived off Norderney Gat. Shortly after, her captain, Nasmith, saw a British seaplane through his periscope and surfaced. The plane landed close by. *E11* took the crew on board and started to tow the seaplane to the carriers' rendezvous area. At 10.00, two more seaplanes were sighted on the water and Nasmith – despite the presence of an enemy Zeppelin – took them on board as well. He opened fire on the undamaged seaplanes to sink them and at the same time, with his crew, waved to the Zeppelin's crew. Fooled into thinking *E11* was a U-boat, the airship made off to attack *D6* which had been seen to dive nearby.

On 4 January 1915, *C31* (Lt G. Pilkington) disappeared when patrolling off Zeebrugge. In the Bight patrol on 18 January, *E10* (Lt-Cdr W. Fraser) also disappeared on the way to her patrol area. Both were probably mined.

British defensive minefields were often more dangerous than those laid by the Germans. They continually broke loose from their moorings and drifted, and as laid the original distance between them was 150 ft – five times the beam of a large U-boat – so had little deterrent effect.

The Dardanelles

Turkey had declared war on 4 November 1914 and the Straits were a formidable 35-mile-long barrier dividing Asia from Europe, giving access to the Sea of Marmara. It narrowed to less than a mile wide between Chanak and Kilid Bahr and was well-protected by five minefields, gun emplacements, forts and searchlights, for the whole length of the coastline. Fitted with special mineguards designed by Lt-Cdr G. N. Pownall who was in charge of the British submarines at Mudros, *B11* (Lt-Cdr N. D. Holbrook) sailed on 1 December 1914, in an attempt to force the Straits and disrupt Turkish naval or merchant ship movements.

These small submarines had already made their way to the Mediterranean on the outbreak of war, under their own power. This was a remarkable feat for small boats only intended for coastal defence. *B11* had also been fitted with new batteries, a major factor in choosing her for this first sortie.

Diving to some 80 ft, the submarine penetrated the uncharted minefields and made her way 11 miles up the Straits to Sari Siglar Bay where she torpedoed the battleship *Messudieh* at a range of 800 yards. In the B Class it will be remembered, the compass was fitted outside the hull to stop it being affected by the metallic bulk of the submarine, and it was read through a reflected image. On the return journey, the lens fogged over and Holbrook had to navigate blind. He and his crew were submerged for nine hours, longer than had been believed possible in such a tiny boat.

The *B11* had twice penetrated five rows of mines; torpedoed a battleship; been navigated underwater without a compass; and remained submerged for nine hours – a tremendous feat of

51

Lt-Cdr N.D. Holbrook, the first VC and Captain of *B11*.

seamanship. Holbrook was awarded the first submarine VC of the war, his No. 1 – Lt S. T. Winn – was awarded the DSO, and the remaining crew members received the DSC or the DSM. Where Holbrook had gone, other submarines could follow and reach the Sea of Marmara to threaten the Turkish lifelines of communication and supply, as had been done in the Baltic. Seven of the E Class and another Australian E Class – designated AE – were chosen for the attacks. It was to become one of the most famous periods in the history of Submarine Command.

On 16 April 1915, *E15* (Lt-Cdr T. S. Brodie) attempted the passage and dived to 80 ft before approaching the minefields. A swift running current swept her ashore near Kephez Point, right under the guns of Fort Dardanus which opened a heavy fire. The Commanding Officer and two others on the bridge were killed by the barrage, and six crew members died from chlorine gas poisoning before the crew surrendered.

The submarine now posed a threat to British security. If she remained in enemy hands, secrets would be revealed to the enemy. *B6* tried to torpedo her but was herself swept ashore near the same point and only escaped after coming under heavy fire. Seaplanes tried to bomb her and other submarines tried to torpedo her, all without success. She was eventually destroyed by two picket boats fitted with torpedo dropping gear, which made a daring night attack.

On 25 April, *AE2* (Lt-Cdr H. H. G. D. Stoker) left Mudros to force the Straits and the next day off Chanak, in the narrowest part of the channel, she torpedoed a Turkish gunboat. Despite heavy surface

The Australian submarine *AE1*.

Two other famous submariners who won the VC in the Dardanelles. Lt-Cdr
E. C. Boyle (left) of *E14* and Lt-Cdr M. Nasmith of *E11*.

attacks, she entered the Sea of Marmara on 25 April, the first British submarine to reach that inland sea.

By 27 April, *E14* (Lt-Cdr E. C. Boyle) was also in the Straits and entered the Sea of Marmara on 29 April, having been submerged for nearly 45 hours, with her batteries almost dead, the air foul and breathing difficult. Boyle torpedoed a troop transport and the two submarines met. *AE2* had fired all her torpedoes at good targets and all had missed. She carried no gun, and never kept the rendezvous the following night having been caught and sunk on the morning of 30 April. In Atarki Bay she had ran into a patch of water with a different density, broke surface and was rammed by a Turkish gunboat. Hit by shells when she resurfaced, Stoker scuttled the boat before he and his crew surrendered.

E14 sank a gunboat and on 10 May off Constantinople, torpedoed a large transport carrying 6,000 troops and a gun battery. The *Gul Djemal* was forced to beach herself to avoid sinking. The enemy was forced to use the long overland route of some 260 miles to supply Gallipoli. This was Boyle's last torpedo and the submarine reached home on 18 May. Boyle was awarded the VC and promoted to Commander for his outstanding achievements. The next day, *E11* (Lt-Cdr M. Nasmith) sailed and by 20 May, was lying on the bottom of the Sea of Marmara waiting for darkness and a chance to recharge batteries.

He captured a small dhow and lashed it alongside the conning-tower so that when trimmed down for diving, only an innocent-looking coastal craft could be seen. Nothing came in sight. On 22 May 1915 off Oxia Island, he chased and torpedoed a transport. He later stopped and sank a small steamer; then chased a transport into the harbour of Rodosto, torpedoed her and set her on fire.

On 25 May he was off Constantinople in the Bosporus and by noon was off the entrance to the harbour itself. The *Stamboul*, a large transport loading stores alongside, was torpedoed. The whole city came to a standstill, with chaos reigning as troops were hurriedly disembarked. All sailings were cancelled.

On 28 May he tried a unique experiment by setting a torpedo to float at the end of its run, instead of sinking if it missed a target. The first time, Nasmith, himself, swam off to carry out the risky job of unscrewing the firing pistol. The torpedo was reloaded through the fore hatch despite the risk involved – the boat would have been unable to dive in an emergency. On all future occasions, the torpedo was taken in through the stern tube. On 6 June he headed back home and torpedoed another transport before arriving back at Imbros after a 20-

day patrol. He was awarded the VC and promoted to commander.

The Es were now refitted with a 6-pdr gun and *E7* (Lt-Cdr A. D. Cochrane) reached the Sea of Marmara on 1 July. On 10 July she torpedoed and sank an ammunition ship and later shelled Constantinople, attacked a train and blew up three ammunition trucks, and returned home after a 24-day patrol having been submerged for the last 11 hours.

E11, now fitted with a 12-pdr gun, sailed on 5 August and after bursting through the nets at a depth of 110 ft, torpedoed a large transport off Nagara Point. On 6 August, *E14* remained on the surface and enticed a Turkish gunboat to attack. The gunboat came within range of the waiting *E11* and was sunk. On 8 August, *E11* torpedoed and sank the *Barbarousse Haireddin*, the last battleship remaining to the Turks.

The first hint of a new Turkish weapon came when *E2* was caught and held in the nets at a depth of 60 ft. Patrol craft attacked her with lance bombs dropped over the side and designed to explode on contact. In the event, the enemy blew a hole in the net and the submarine escaped. *E11* returned to Mudros on 4 September 1915 in a blaze of glory, having torpedoed three transports found at anchor, and sunk the fourth which had got under weigh, on her way home.

That same day, *E7* was caught and held firmly in nets at a depth of 100 ft and was attacked by a crude form of depth-charge, now set to go off at a predetermined depth. A violent explosion plunged the boat into darkness and there was no chance of escape. After destroying confidential documents and fixing the scuttling charges, the submarine surfaced and surrendered.

E12 (Lt-Cdr K. M. Bruce) was involved in a similar incident but miraculously escaped. She broke through some nets but a portion got entangled in the fore hydroplanes and the submarine took on a steep diving angle. She passed 100 ft, then 150 ft, 200 ft and finally levelled off at 245 ft – deeper than any British submarine had ever dived before. Glass scuttles cracked under the tremendous pressure and the conning-tower flooded. The pressure hull started leaking. After 10 minutes at 245 ft, the submarine started to surface rapidly. The conning-tower broke surface and she was fired on and hit by shore batteries, but after a remarkable voyage, reached home safely.

Yet a further example will serve to pinpoint the dangers faced by these submariners. *E20* (Lt-Cdr C. H. Warren) fitted with a 6-inch howitzer met the French submarine *Turquoise* at a secret rendezvous, and arranged to meet her again. The *Turquoise* ran ashore and was captured intact, together with the secret papers giving details of the meeting. *E20* kept the rendezvous and was torpedoed by *UB14* as she lay on the surface waiting for her French ally.

These were but a few of the major events in the Dardanelles campaign during which coastal traffic had been virtually stopped; two battleships, one destroyer, five gunboats, nine transports, 30 smaller craft, seven ammunition and supply ships, together with 188 sailing vessels, had been sunk. Three VCs had been won. Britain had lost five submarines.

Other Developments

Although the Baltic and Dardanelles campaigns proved the strategic value of submarines, unrestricted warfare as announced by the Germans on 4 February 1915, added a new dimension to the threat. They even attacked unarmed fishing boats in the North Sea, using them for gunnery target practice. Clearly this could not be allowed to continue. The intensification of anti-submarine warfare led to the use of vessels disguised as trawlers – but each armed with a gun – known as Q-boats. Another tactic was developed by the submarines at Leith, where they were 'mothered' by HMS *Vulcan*. The idea was to tow a small submarine at a depth of 40 ft behind a trawler. When a U-boat surfaced to attack the fishing fleet, the submarine would slip its tow, manoeuvre into position for an attack and torpedo the U-boat on the surface. This also demanded communications between the trawler and submarine, solved by a telephone cable. Trials proved successful even allowing for the extra weight of 600 ft of 3.5 inch wire rope, 8-inch hawser and telephone cable.

On 23 June, the trawler *Taranaki* (Lt-Cdr Edwards), towing *C24* (Lt Taylor) was with a group of fishing boats near the Dogger Bank when a U-boat surfaced in the middle of the fleet. She selected the *Taranaki* as her first victim and fired a shot across her bows. The slip gear on the submarine jammed and the tow was slipped by the trawler instead. Burdened with all this extra weight and a bow-down angle of five degrees, Taylor nevertheless worked his way into an attacking position at periscope depth and torpedoed *U40* amidships. There were only two survivors recovered by *C24* which now had the telephone cable wrapped round her propeller and was unable to move. The cable was eventually cleared and *C24* returned to harbour.

On 20 July 1915, this success was repeated by the trawler *Princess Louise* (Lt Cantlie) and the *C27* (Lt-Cdr Dobson). The *U23* surfaced 2,500 yards on the port bow of the trawler and opened fire. This time

Lt R. D. Sandford, who was awarded the VC in 1918 after the old *C3* packed with explosives blew the Mole at Zeebrugge to pieces.

H.28

L.12

6351

Three submarines of the war years in dock together at Barrow. *L12* and *H28* were representative of two well-proven types and the *R7* (right) was one of a later class developed towards the end of the war.

the telephone to the submarine broke down. On hearing the shells hit the water, however, *C27* slipped her tow successfully and eased her way to within 500 yards of the enemy before firing a torpedo. At the same time, the U-boat started her engines and the first shot passed astern. Shifting deflection, *C27* fired her starboard tube and hit the enemy aft of the conning-tower. Seven survivors including the Captain were picked up by *C27* which returned to port. This was the last success by this means of attack. As the news spread among the U-boat Captains the attacks on the fishing fleets ceased, and as this had been a major reason for the tactic in the first place, it must be considered as another success for Submarine Command.

When the German U-boats returned to raiding the fishing fleet in 1916, no new methods had been devised for combating them and the towed submarine was again used. Conditions were now very different, however, as the North Sea was heavily mined and small groups of mines were continually being laid by U-boats. In early August working with the trawler *Malta*, *C33* was relieved by another C Class and set course for harbour. She was never seen again. On 29 August came another disaster when *C29* (Lt Schofield) was being towed submerged by the *Ariadne* off the entrance to the Humber. *C29* was towed into a minefield and was lost with all hands. Clearly the towed-decoy tactic was too dangerous to continue. It was abandoned and the Q-boats were used – trawlers and fishing smacks, each with a concealed gun.

Another epic achievement was by the oldest of the class, *C3* (Lt R. D. Sandford), which was chosen to take part in the raid on Zeebrugge, St George's Day, 1918. She was fitted with automatic steering, was packed full of explosives, and carried a crew of two officers and seven ratings. She was to wedge her bows under the viaduct connecting the Mole to the mainland and blow it and herself to pieces. She got into position perfectly, watched by hundreds of enemy soldiers who just could not credit what was happening. Sandford lit the fuze connected to the dynamite packed in the bows and the crew scrambled into their small motor boat. The Germans recovered from their shock and opened a heavy fire. The motor boat propeller was hit and put out of action so two of the crew grabbed two paddles and started to try and put as much distance as possible between the submarine and themselves. They were wounded almost immediately, and were replaced by two others. When about 600 ft clear, the *C3* exploded violently and the soldiers lining the viaduct, reinforcements rushing to the fighting on the Mole, were blown to pieces. By this time the boat was holed and sinking fast and only one crew member was unwounded. Just in time, the crew were taken off by a naval picket boat the crew of which included Sandford's brother. Sandford was awarded the VC.

So many new designs for submarines were put forward that in May 1915, a Submarine Development Committee was formed to consider future policy and they quickly arrived at six types. They decided to continue the existing coastal and the overseas types, which were bearing the brunt of the war. Fleet submarines were thought necessary but future developments were left until after the *K1* trials. Minelayers were already in existence and could be continued if there was a Naval Staff Requirement. Submarine monitors were also thought necessary as it was believed that a submarine with a 12-inch gun could find plenty of action in the North Sea, with an added element of surprise. Lord Fisher favoured monitors because the low speed of the torpedo – some 24 knots – did not allow for errors against high-speed surface targets taking evasive action.

One of the strangest prizes ever to fall to a submarine was the Zeppelin *L7* on 4 May 1916. *E31* (Lt-Cdr Feilman) was working with some minelayers and the seaplane carriers *Vixden* and *Engadine*. When *E31* surfaced she saw a Zeppelin overhead and made an emergency dive to get out of the way. There were no bombs. Coming back to periscope depth, the Captain saw the Zeppelin, apparently in difficulties and low down. He surfaced, went to gun stations, and shot it down by gunfire. He brought seven survivors home with him.

The race to be the first minelaying E Class went to *E24* (Lt-Cdr Napier), which sailed on 4 March 1916 for the mouth of the Elbe. The submarine covered some 750 miles on the surface and 20 miles submerged in 60 hours. She returned to Harwich on 10 March. Any submarine operating in the Bight or for that matter the North Sea, faced a very dangerous situation. For the minelayers it was doubly dangerous. They not only had to find the enemy's secret swept channels and lay mines in them to 'confound' the enemy, but had to lay mines in the approaches to heavily defended enemy harbours. The *E24* disappeared on her next trip.

On 19 August *E23* (Lt-Cdr R. Turner) sighted the German Fleet off Borkum Riff at 03.00 and attacked the battle-cruiser *Seydlitz* from 800 yards and missed. The second wave of ships was attacked with two bow tubes and the battleship *Westfalen* was hit by a torpedo which tore a hole in her side. Although listing heavily, she reached port without sinking.

On 19 October 1916, *E38* (Lt-Cdr Jessop) torpedoed the light cruiser *Munchen*, but she still managed to reach a home port. On 5 November in *J1*, off Horns Riff and in a heavy swell, Cdr Laurence sighted four battleships and although he broke surface and dived sharply, he fired his bow tubes and scored hits on the *Kronprinz* and the *Grosser Kurfurst*.

Just watching an empty waste of sea with orders not to attack but report, as in the Bight, must have seemed a terrible ordeal for dedicated submariners anxious to attack the enemy. *H5* commanded by Lieutenant Varley was one who strayed from the straight and narrow off his patrol area near Terschelling on 11 July 1916. The following morning he was off Borkum near the enemy coast when it was found that one periscope was very difficult to turn. That night, *H5* surfaced to recharge batteries and do repairs. A destroyer attacked and the submarine had to dive swiftly, leaving all the special tools on the upper deck to be swept away.

On 13 July he attacked some destroyers but all the torpedoes missed. The next morning, however, *U51* was sighted leaving for her patrol position. Despite the short, steep and choppy seas which made it difficult to maintain an even diving position, *H5* closed to 600 yards and torpedoed the submarine which sank without trace.

British submarines were also busy in the Adriatic, the Mediterranean and north of the Canary Islands where *E35* (Lt-Cdr D'Oyly Hughes) covered 22,000 miles during routine patrols of 22 days at sea followed by 10 days in harbour. For her the excitement mounted when Naval Intelligence learned that two German submarines were to keep a rendezvous off Cape St Vincent. *E35* left Gibraltar to try and keep the same 'appointment' and on 11 May 1918 was in position. Despite the difficult sea conditions she sighted a large submarine that afternoon. The enemy turned away leaving *E35* with a long and difficult stern chase which lasted for two hours. When *E35* put up her extra-long periscope, the enemy had just turned back and was passing very close. The first torpedo passed beneath her. At 18.00 that evening, the enemy altered course again, and closing to within 400 yards, the *E35* fired two torpedoes. Both hit and the *U154*, one of the German Navy's largest underwater cruisers, disappeared forever.

Shortly after the outbreak of war in November 1914, 20 submarines were ordered from the American steel giants, the Bethlehem Corporation, and were turned over to the Electric Boat Company. But in order to avoid breaking the neutrality 'laws', parts for 10 of them (*H1–10*) were sent to Vickers, Montreal, V. (Mont) for completion. Eventually 14 were delivered (*H1–12, 14* and *15*), and the other eight remained at the Fore River Yard, Quincy, USA (Fore R).

In 1917, *H13* and *H16–20* were ceded to the Chilean Navy as replacements for warships taken over in 1914. *H14* and *15* went to the

Royal Canadian Navy in 1919.

The British H21 Class were a modification of the original American H Class design with a heavier torpedo armament. Instead of four 18-inch, they had four 21-inch bow tubes and the overall length was increased by 21 ft and surface displacement to 438 ton. Like the original Hs, they had a crew of 22. They were the first twin screw, single-hulled boats in the Royal Navy and were powered by American-designed diesels producing 480 hp, driving them at 11.5 knots on the surface. The American-designed main motors powered by 120 battery cells, produced 620 bhp for one hour and 320 bhp continuously, for a submerged speed of 9 knots. In service they averaged 9 miles at 8 knots and 34 miles at 3.5 knots submerged.

In 1916 the Admiralty decided to return to the saddle-tank type of submarine with the design for a bigger and improved E Class incorporating the lessons already learned during the war. In the February, two were ordered from Vickers and numbered *E57* and *58*. These were such an improvement, in both design and concept, that it was decided to give them a class letter of their own. *E57* and *58* were given the class title of L, and the two Es were renumbered as *L1* and *L2*. The class can be divided into three distinct groups. *L1–8* were armed with four 18-inch bow and two beam tubes. *L9–33* had four 21-inch bow tubes and two 18-inch beam tubes. Later *L14, 17* and *24–27* were fitted out as minelayers with 21-inch bow tubes. In addition to torpedoes, they were armed with a gun just forward of the conning-tower. *L1–8* were fitted with a 3-inch high-angle anti-aircraft gun, but eventually all were fitted with a 4-inch. This meant increasing the crew from 35 to 38, but still the submarines only carried one small collapsible lifeboat.

By December of 1917, 34 L Class had been ordered but only 27 actually commissioned for operational service, with *L13* never ordered because of superstition; *L28–32* were never completed and *L34* and *35* were cancelled. Vickers built 18 of this type.

The Ls were also the first British submarines designed to carry some 20 ton of their normal fuel tonnage in two specially built external tanks and began the practice, later developed during the 1920s, of carrying fuel externally. Two 12-cylinder diesels developed a total of 2,400 bhp at 380 rpm, to give a surface speed of just over 17 knots. Three battery tanks each of 112 cells could be worked at 220 v. in series or 110 v. in parallel, driving four main motors of the shunt-wound double-armature type, to give 1,600 bhp at 300 rpm for a submerged speed of 10.5 knots. A 20-hp auxiliary motor could be used for slow running of 1.75 knots submerged.

They were excellent boats, sturdy and well built. Although the official maximum depth (1925) was given as 150 ft, depending on age and construction, depths of more than 250 ft were recorded and during one uncontrolled dive, *L2* reached a depth of 300 ft and survived unharmed. Only one was lost during the war and that was *L10*, sunk by a German destroyer off Texel in 1918.

Later, the L Class was modified to incorporate a better armament and were known as the L50 Class, but only seven were completed. All the remainder were sold, the last three in 1939.

Another special design of this period was the small R Class, the first British submarine ever designed as a 'killer' of enemy submarines, and the forerunner of the British nuclear-powered Fleet submarines such as HMS *Conqueror*, which torpedoed and sank the heavily armoured Argentine cruiser, the *General Belgrano*, during the Falkland Crisis which started with their invasion on 2 April 1982.

The R Class only displaced 420 ton on the surface, but submerged they were powered by a K Class battery generating 1,200 bhp. The streamlined hull and conning-tower, and a minimum of superstructure, gave them an underwater speed of 15 knots. It was a record that remained intact until near the end of the Second World War.

They were also the first submarines, like the *Conqueror*, to mount a salvo of six bow tubes with 18-inch torpedoes (*Conqueror* the 21-inch Tigerfish). During the war, six spares were stowed in the Senior Rates' Mess of the R Class – it has not yet been revealed where they slept! The Rs also had a submerged range of 150 miles at their 'creep' speed of 1.5 knots, and 15 miles at full power – a range greater than that of any other British submarine. Completed in 1918, these beautifully designed boats saw very little service and were all sold in 1923. Stealth technology and submerged speed were ignored, and the major efforts of submarine designers were directed to faster surface speeds, bigger gun armaments, and an ability to operate with the Fleet under operational conditions. All were doomed to failure as was the case with the K Class, and the Ms which followed.

The problem of finding and then 'killing' the enemy was almost solved by the five hydrophones operated by them. These simple devices, making use of the fact that sound in water could be heard over very long distances, became more sensitive and directional as the war went on. They were designed to register the submarine propeller revolving in the water and it was found – like the null in direction finding by wireless – that the most accurate bearing was obtained when a minimum of sound was heard through the headphones. As soon as a propeller was heard, the hydrophone was rotated until the sound disappeared or was minimal, and the bearing for attack was 90 degrees – right angles to the bearing given by the hydrophone.

The war also saw the development of the high-powered underwater depth-charge, where the depth of the explosion was controlled by a hydrostatic valve. This in turn, led to designers building submarines with stronger hulls to withstand shock and deeper diving, and watertight doors to shut off damaged compartments as in surface ships. Set up towards the end of the war, the Anti-Submarine Detection Investigation Committee (ASDIC), developed what was basically a quartz plate – similar to the crystal used in generating radio transmissions – and when an electric current was passed through it, it vibrated at a set frequency. These supersonic waves could be transmitted directionally and when they came into contact with an underwater mass such as a submarine, they were reflected back to the receiver. Knowing the speed of sound in water, the time between sending and receiving enabled the attacker to calculate the range of the submarine, and mount an attack. Besides use in surface ships the apparatus could be installed in submarines and enable them to attack enemy surface vessels or submarines.

Surface ships, however, had no way yet of finding out the depth of a submarine and at best the system only provided a range. But, happily for the British, the Germans then had no knowledge of the developments and the potential of the ASDIC remained unknown to them until the war was almost over.

The last time a submarine was in contact with the German Fleet of the First World War was on 21 April 1918, when *E42* (Lt-Cdr Allen), fixing a position in the setting sun of the evening, sighted a division of German battle-cruisers with some light cruisers. He attacked at extreme range – with no hits – but then, unexpectedly, there arrived the battle-cruiser *Moltke*. She had engine trouble and was escorted by three torpedo boats. The submarine fired one torpedo which hit the *Moltke* astern, and put her out of action for 18 months.

On 12 November 1918, after the Armistice was signed, Commodore (S) S. S. Hall issued a general message to his command congratulating them on sinking 54 enemy warships, and 274 other vessels – a magnificent achievement.

Losses attributed to mining by submarines were 23 merchant ships and one U-boat in British waters; 12 merchant ships, a destroyer, three torpedo boats and a corvette in the Mediterranean; and three merchant ships in the Far East.

The 'Kalamity Kays'

It was in the spring of 1913 that Sir Eustace Tennyson-d'Eyncourt, then Director of Naval Construction, produced the design for a steam-driven submarine that was to be bigger than many British destroyers. The design was not taken up but by December 1914 rumours were circulating in high naval circles that some German submarines were capable of 19 knots, and that the British Fleet ought to have high-speed submarines capable of operating with them. The idea of a Fleet submarine was born.

In December 1914, however, the French steam-driven *Archimède*, operating in the Heligoland Bight, was damaged by heavy seas which buckled her funnel and prevented it being lowered for diving. Water poured in through the funnel opening and the crew, including a British liaison officer Lt-Cdr Godfrey Herbert, had to bail out the boiler room. Come dawn, she was still on the surface unable to dive and it was more than two days later before she crawled slowly into Harwich. Fisher said he wanted to hear no more of steam engines and submarines.

Both the *Nautilus*, an experimental diesel-engined type capable of 17 knots, and the steam-driven *Swordfish*, designed for 19 knots, were still on the stocks but the heavy building programme had delayed work on them by Vickers and Scotts. The Admiralty opted for the diesel-powered J Class, designed for 21 knots. They used three E-type engines with 36 cylinders and on 29 January 1915, an order for eight was placed with Portsmouth, Devonport and Chatham Dockyards.

Meantime Keyes and Fisher were not seeing eye to eye on the building programme. Keyes said that Vickers had been given orders for overseas submarines up to their full building capacity. On 25 May 1915, Sir Trevor Dawson, then managing director of Vickers, had told Fisher that the company would soon be sacking workmen for want of orders. While the Baltic and Dardanelles campaigns were in progress, Fisher recalled S. S. Hall and appointed him as Commodore (S) in place of Keyes, who went to the Dardanelles as Chief Staff Officer. Earlier, in March, Hall had told Fisher that the Js could only do 19 knots and were too slow to operate with the Fleet.

The Admiralty were now forced to reconsider steam as a motive power and d'Eyncourt's 1913 design was compared with that of Vickers, and ideas from both were incorporated in the K Class, including an auxiliary diesel engine for safety reasons.

These huge vessels were the most bizarre submarines ever built and *K3*, laid down by the King in 1915, was the first to commission on 4

The submarine *K3*, with smoke swirling from her twin funnels, punches her way through a heavy sea which completely obliterates her bows.

August 1916. Although 28 were ordered in batches, only 17 were completed. Vickers built six at an estimated cost of £340,000. Others were built by Fairfield, Armstrong-Whitworth, Scotts, Beardmore, Portsmouth and Devonport Dockyards.

These huge underwater cruisers were the fastest and biggest submarines in the world, with a length of 330 ft and a beam of 26.5 ft, displacing 2,566 ton submerged. Their phenomenal speed of 24 knots was provided by oil-fired steam turbines, driving twin screws through double helical gearing. There were nine watertight doors, many valves, and ten 18-inch torpedo tubes – four bow, four beam and two on deck though the latter were soon removed.

The twin 5 ft high funnels behind the streamlined superstructure were raised and lowered by an electric motor and hinged to fold down

69

into watertight wells. The holes left in the superstructure were closed by hatches which operated with the funnels. Holes where the funnels passed through the pressure hull were closed by hatches operated by motors and clipped by hand from inside the submarine.

The submarines had to be operated by 'remote control'. There were nine compartments and the boiler room virtually split the submarine in half, the two being joined by a narrow tunnel. Two 30-ft periscopes – the largest then fitted to a British submarine – and two radio masts were also fitted. After trials in *K3*, the enclosed boiler room was fitted with extra fans to mitigate the tremendous heat developed which made the space an 'airless oven'. The narrow passageway linking the two halves of the submarine was also added so the engine room crew could get a breather.

The boiler-room air vents were closed by hydraulics and there were two high-power compressors to charge the 4 ft-long steel containers known as 'bottles'. Hydraulic rams raised the periscopes and telescopic masts, and the hydroplanes were operated by hydroelectric controls.

The sharp bows stood 9 ft clear of the water and at 12 knots or more lacked buoyancy and sliced through the sea sending torrents of water over the foredeck making it impossible to man the gun. Behind the canvas screen which served as a protection for those conning the submarine from the bridge, the job was unpleasant and often dangerous. The large, flat surface of the foredeck resulted in an alarming tendency to dive by acting as a hydroplane and increasing the downward thrust.

Even more bizarre, the underside of the fuel tanks were open to the sea and the oil literally floated on the water and was drawn by pumps from the top of the tanks. In calm seas this self-compensating system worked well, but in a rough sea, oil and water tended to emulsify and this mixture put out the boiler fires. In *K2* during acceptance trials, the icy water partly solidified the oil in the hydraulics and nearly caused a disaster. Thereafter, all Ks were ordered to use Arctic grade non-freezing oil.

Double-hulled, the Ks had 20 main external ballast tanks in the lower parts of the two hulls, with further ballast and trimming tanks in the bottom of the hull. 'Too many damned holes', as one submariner said. Nevertheless, they could submerge faster than any previous steam-driven submarine, and although 30 seconds was the maximum time allowed for lowering and securing the funnels, they still took an impossibly long 5 minutes to submerge. The fastest time ever recorded was 3 minutes 25 seconds by *K8*. Two 10-ton keels, one fore and one aft, could be released in an emergency. Surface endurance was 960 miles at full speed and 12,500 miles at 10 knots. Submerged endurance was 30 miles at 4 knots. The crew of 59 had no escape apparatus.

The trail of disasters began early in the life of the Ks. On her speed trials *K3* had a wheel-house window smashed by heavy seas and was fired on by a 'friendly' patrol craft off the Isle of Man. Later, Cdr Edward Leir took the Prince of Wales (later King George VI) and C-in-C Portsmouth for a dive in Stokes Bay. *K3* refused to catch a trim and stuck her bows in the mud 150 ft down while her stern stuck out of the water with propellers spinning wildly. It was 20 minutes before she surfaced. Later, on 9 January 1917, heavy seas cascaded down both funnels and put out the boiler fires. As she lost way, more water crashed down the funnels partly flooding the boiler room. She used her auxiliary diesel to return to harbour.

On 18 January 1917, *K13* did 23.5 knots on her speed trials and on 29 January, Commander Godfrey Herbert prepared her for a final dive in Gare Loch. Built by Fairfield Shipbuilding & Engineering Company in 15 months, the giant submarine had 80 men on board including civilians from the shipbuilders and Commander Francis Goodhart, captain designate of *K14*, also being built by Fairfield.

At 20 ft it was reported that the boiler room was flooding freely and although main ballast tanks were blown and the 10-ton forward keel dropped, she continued out of control to the seabed 50 ft below. Aft of the torpedo room, the submarine was completely flooded and 31 men drowned.

Helped by Herbert, Goodhart made a gallant escape attempt through the conning-tower. After flooding to equalize pressures inside and out, high-pressure air was used to blow him to the surface in an air bubble. Goodhart drowned in the attempt but Herbert, swept off his feet by the upward rush of air, miraculously reached the outside and surfaced safely. Earlier in his submarine career as Captain of *D5* he had also escaped when the boat struck a mine and the explosion blew him clear of the conning-tower.

It was 57 hours later that the remainder of the crew were able to escape via a hole cut through both hulls by an oxy-acetylene torch. Six weeks later, this ill-fated submarine was raised and renumbered *K22*. Fairfield never built another submarine after *K14*. No other submarine was ever numbered 13, and few of the survivors ever set foot in one again. At a subsequent Admiralty Inquiry, divers reported finding four 37-inch ventilators over the boiler room open, indicators in the boiler room set open, and the engine-room hatch undone.

K4 started her career by going aground at Walney Island, off

An omen for the K Class? *K4* left high and dry after going aground on her way from the yard at Barrow.

Barrow. *K2* caught fire during early trials in a dockyard basin off Portsmouth Harbour – there were no fire extinguishers on board.

On 18 November 1917, the 12th Flotilla of Ks were out with the Fleet for a sweep off Denmark. During a sharply executed turning manoeuvre, *K4* rammed *K1* and crippled her so much that the flotilla leader HMS *Blonde* had to sink her by gunfire. About this time too, some of the Ks were retro-fitted with large swan bows in which were fitted quick-blowing buoyancy tanks.

The refitted *K13*, now *K22*, joined the 13th Flotilla in Scotland and the scene was set for what has become known as the 'Battle of May Island'. In the submarine *K6* was a young midshipman, Lord Francis Albert Victor Nicholas Mountbatten. The Rosyth force of 3 battleships, 4 battle-cruisers, 14 light cruisers, the Ks and destroyers, left Rosyth on 31 January 1918. Forty warships were to be taken through the narrow and congested waters of the Forth to meet up with Beatty's force from Scapa Flow, in the North Sea.

The Rosyth force sailed in darkness, under radio silence and showing only one stern light. The Ks were some 400 yards apart showing single, blue stern lights at half brilliance and shaded by screens to prevent them being seen except from 11 degrees off the centre-line astern.

HMS *Ithuriel* led *K11, 17, 14, 12* and *22*. HMS *Fearless* led *K4, 3, 6* and *7* in that order. The Isle of May is just beyond the tips of the estuary where the warships were due to increase speed from 19 to 21 knots. They ran into a low-lying mist and visibility for ordinary, brilliant stern lights was reduced to a mile.

To those in *K14*, it seemed that *K11*, followed by *K17*, reduced speed and hauled out of line. *K14* reduced to 13 knots but held her course. *K22* lost sight of the stern light of *K12* ahead, but at 19 knots rammed *K14*. Both submarines were badly flooded forward.

Four ships of the 2nd Battle-Cruiser Squadron led by HMS *Inflexible*, bore down on the two flooded submarines from astern, and the *Inflexible* smashed into *K22* at 18 knots. By a miracle, both submarines remained afloat.

Meanwhile, the *Ithuriel* had picked up the distress call and turned back to help in any rescue required, followed by *K12*, astern of *K17*. Suddenly, ahead of the *Ithuriel*, appeared the battle-cruisers, and astern of them the *Fearless* leading the other K-boats. The *Fearless* slammed into *K17* at 21 knots, and on a calm sea the submarine sank slowly beneath the surface.

In the general confusion *K4* was rammed by *K6* which cut the other submarine almost in two and sank her. In a few hours, two Ks had

been sunk, with two more and the *Fearless* badly damaged.

The near disasters, however, were not yet over. On 2 May 1918, *K3* trimmed for diving in the Pentland Firth, got out of control and hit the bottom at a depth of 266 ft. She surfaced safely although stays and plates were crumpled by the pressure.

Remarkably, on 10 June 1918, the Admiralty ordered a further six K Class boats, *K23–28*.

The *K26* deserves mention. Laid down at Vickers in June 1918, she was launched some 14 months later and towed to Chatham where she completed in June 1923. Armed with six 21-inch bow tubes, she had an increased displacement of 2,140 ton surfaced and was 351 ft long. A major advance was the introduction of battery compartments – later to become standard in all British submarines. Her diving depth was given as 250 ft. In 1924 she made a world cruise to Gibraltar, Malta, through the Red Sea to Colombo, Singapore and return. She was scrapped in April 1931.

On 20 January 1921, *K5, 8, 9, 15* and *22* were anchored at Tor Bay with the Fleet ready for manoeuvres, and sailed for the exercise battle zone. The next morning the mock battle began and the submarines spread out to attack as an 'enemy cruiser' came into sight. *K5* dived first and was never seen again. Pieces of wreckage recovered from the scene all came from the control room which had proved to be the weakest part of the pressure hull in the K Class. On 25 June 1921, *K15* sank alongside HMS *Canterbury* in the tidal basin at Portsmouth. Salvaged 13 days later, she was beached on the mud flats near Whale Island and was eventually scrapped in 1923.

Many of the naval hierarchy favoured the idea of a submersible battleship, no doubt worried by the German U-boat cruisers armed with 5.9-inch guns. Lord Fisher submitted a proposal after his resignation to the then First Lord, Lord Balfour. Submitted on 5 August 1915, the proposal was to mount a 60-ton 12-inch gun from a battleship in front of the conning-tower. The operation entailed searching for a target at the periscope depth of 30 ft. Once in sight, the submarine was lined up accurately with the target with the gun elevated at the appropriate angle. When about 6 ft of the gun barrel was above the surface, the gun would be fired and the submarine would submerge. It was argued that the 850-lb shells were cheaper than torpedoes, and some 40 could be carried on one patrol. The element of surprise was also considered of strategic importance.

The scheme was eventually approved with orders for two each being placed with Vickers and Armstrong Whitworth using the keels of *K18, 19, 20* and *21*. The M Class were part double-hulled with the double hull extending for some 65 per cent of the overall length, which after some modifications turned out to be 305 ft, with a beam of 24.5 feet. A surface speed of 15 knots was achieved on trials using two Vickers-designed 12-cylinder diesels, each of 1,200 bhp. Submerged, she was driven by four double-armature motors each generating 400 bhp to reach a speed of 9 knots. Power was supplied by three battery tanks each of 112 Exide cells.

The boat behaved impeccably and could dive in 30 seconds. The gun proved very reliable even after being underwater for several hours.

The firing and submerging operation took 55 seconds. The designed endurance was 2,500 miles on the surface at 16 knots or 4,500 miles at an economical cruising speed. Submerged endurance was 10 miles at 10 knots. Diving depth was 200 ft. The propellers were 5 ft 10 in in diameter and had three blades.

Although the orders were placed for the first of the class in February 1916, it was not until April 1918 that *M1* (Vickers) was ready for operations. That famous submariner Max Horton took *M1* to the Mediterranean but never fired a shot in anger. After the war to conform with the Washington Disarmament Treaty of 1920 which said no submarine could have a gun larger than an 8-inch, *M2* and *M3* had their guns removed. *M2* was refitted with a seaplane hangar replacing the gun and a catapult to launch a small Parnall Peto seaplane, which had an endurance of two hours at 70 knots. In 1927, *M3* was converted to an experimental minelayer, with 100 mines on rails inside a free-flooding casing outside the hull. A conveyor belt laid the mines over the stern. She functioned perfectly. Originally they were armed with four 18-inch bow tubes but in *M3* these were replaced with four 21-inch, and a subsequent increase in length to 305 ft, 10 ft longer than the others. *M4* was never completed but the calamity of the Ks remained with the class.

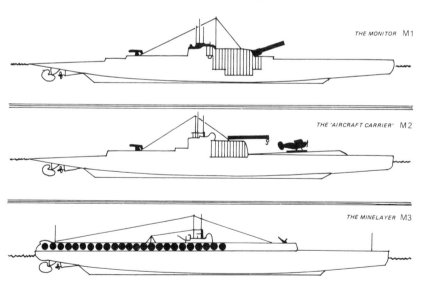

THE MONITOR M1

THE 'AIRCRAFT CARRIER' M2

THE MINELAYER M3

Between the wars, ocean-going submarines of the O, P and R Classes, as well as submarine minelayers were built.

This is HMS *Perseus*, completed in 1930 and lost in the Mediterranean in 1941.

Take-off from an A Class submarine.

On 12 November 1925, the *M1* dived some 15 miles off Start Point and was never seen again. Ten days later, a Swedish coaster *Vidar* arrived at the Kiel Canal and reported ramming a submerged object off Start Point. Her bottom plates were buckled and had traces of grey-green camouflage paint. The crew of 69 perished. This was the fourth submarine disaster in peacetime, since the end of the war. On 23 March 1922, HMS *Versatile* rammed and sank the obsolete *H42*, killing 26 men. On 10 January 1924, the battleship *Resolution* rammed and sank *L24* off Portland Bill, killing 43 crew. On 26 January 1932, the *M2* dived off Portland and disappeared. Shortly afterwards *M3* was scrapped. The last of the K boats, *K26* was scrapped in March 1931 – the final end of the 'Kalamity Kays'.

Many famous submariners who also served in the class survived to reach high rank in the Navy including: Admiral Sir Geoffrey Layton (*K6*); Vice-Admiral Sir Robert Ross-Turner (*K8*); Rear-Admiral W. Leir (*K3* and CO 13th Flotilla); Rear-Admiral Allan Poland (*K22* and *K26*); Captains Hubert Vaughan Jones (*K6* and *K15*), G. Herbert (*K13*), R. L. Mackenzie Edwards (*K22*); and Commanders S. G. Gravener (*K7* and *K16*), J. C. Harbottle (*K14*), L. C. Rideal (*K13*), C. Stevens (*K22*) and J. G. Sutton (*K3*).

3
A SECOND RISING

After the war, Submarine Command entered upon yet another phase in its development as the lessons of war were digested and new designs were suggested.

The submarine had become a lone-wolf weapon of great strategic importance, though its tactical value was, to all intents and purposes, minimal. Although vulnerable to improved counter-measures, it had great endurance, greater diving depths and could kill with a single shot.

It was not so flexible in operations as a surface warship as the 'bridge' was low down in the water with a much reduced horizon distance. The so-called 'Battle of the Bight' had shown quite clearly the confusion that could arise when operating with the surface fleet, and the disaster with the K Class must have hammered home that very point.

By the end of 1919, 10 As, 27 Cs, and 3 Ds were scrapped and in the years to 1924, they were joined by 29 Es, the Fs, Gs and some Hs.

During the period between the wars, there was no major threat to Britain's naval superiority until Hitler came to power. Except for the Japanese, all the maritime powers were going through an economic depression and the future role of the battleship was under discussion. With even the most modern battleships vulnerable to modern guns, there was a powerful lobby that argued for their abolition with new construction centred on small, fast cruisers, destroyers, aircraft-carriers and submarines.

Britain repeatedly tried to get the submarine banned. She tried at Versailles in 1919, at Washington in 1921, and in London during 1931. All without success. It was agreed at last that the submarine could be used only in 'accordance with the laws and customs of war' – whatever that rather trite phrase might have meant. The Root Resolutions, Washington, re-affirmed that the submarine was not exempt from the rule of visit and search, before seizure.

The big ship partisans were resolutely opposed to the submarine yet forgot that the submarine had posed a threat to merchant shipping greater than that posed by powerful German-armed merchant raiders. The Royal Naval Tactical School was formed in 1925 to assess many of the lessons of the war, but too little time appears to have been devoted to the prolonged submarine warfare waged against allied merchantmen. The Fighting Instructions of 1924 and 1928 were still primarily concerned with Fleet actions. The anti-submarine lobby argued that once dived, although it could mount an attack unseen, the submarine lost tactical mobility – being unable to maintain contact with a convoy for more than the one attack and having to use up its limited supply of torpedoes, rather than rely on the gun.

Operational use of the ASDIC for submarine detection was gradually built up between the wars. Winston Churchill, who had expressed doubts about Britain's anti-submarine warfare capabilities, was taken on a visit to Portland. He was moved to declare afterwards that anti-submarine measures had developed out of all recognition – a statement hardly justified by the results obtained in tests and the limited performance of the ASDIC apparatus on which so much faith was pinned. HMS *Winchelsea*, in a series of 250 attacks by submarines of the 6th Flotilla, obtained an average detection range of 1,800 yards and detected 80 per cent of the submarines during attacks. But, importantly, not in time for her to have taken avoiding action against torpedoes.

The 1921–2 Naval Estimates included the order for *X1*, which was the largest submarine in the world when completed in 1925 at Chatham. Displacing 2,780 ton surfaced and 3,600 ton submerged, she was 363.5 ft long, 29.75 ft in the beam, and was driven on the surface by two huge 3,000 hp diesels at a speed of 19.5 knots. Carrying a crew of 102, she was armed with six 21-inch torpedo tubes in the bows, and four 5.2-inch guns in twin turrets. Like most British experimental designs, however, there were frequent technical faults, particularly with the engines, and she was finally scrapped in 1936 after a period in reserve. The design was never carried through and only the one submarine was built.

Meanwhile, the Allied Submarine Detection Investigation Committee, in which Britain played a leading part, had come up with the improved ASDIC device to give greater punch to anti-submarine warfare. As an added bonus it also allowed submarines to talk to each other at ranges of up to 7 miles. Though, despite being sensitive and directional, the enemy U-boats could listen in of course.

The first of the British submarines to be fitted with ASDIC were those of the larger and more powerful O Class, the first of the early post-war designs, and were ordered in the 1924 programme. The seven were *Oberon, Odin, Olympus, Orpheus, Osiris, Oswald* and *Otus*. Two others of the class, *Oxley* and *Otway*, were built for the Royal Australian Navy, but subsequently returned to the Royal Navy. It was felt that the L Class, which was the Command's main strength at the

The Australian submarine *Otway*.

time, did not have enough endurance for the Far East. Consequently, the Os had greater bunkerage giving them an estimated endurance of 6,500 miles at 10 knots on the surface. The extra 200 ton of fuel needed for this range was carried in the riveted exterior saddle tanks, and these proved to have one of their few faults. Oil did occasionally leak from them to leave a visible slick of oil on the surface of the water.

The class was fitted with the Type 118 ASDIC – the hydrophone disappeared – and the pressure hulls were greatly strengthened. Another innovation was the fitting of 40-ft periscopes to take them deep enough at periscope depth to avoid ramming by a surface vessel.

During the building of the first submarine, there was an unexpected growth in top 'hamper' to cope with new technology, and on completion in 1927 it was doubted if her designed underwater speed of 9 knots from twin motors developing 1,320 bhp would be obtained. On trials she managed 7.5 knots. The Admiralty-designed diesels in *Oberon* gave 2,700 bhp and a surface speed of 13.5 knots, but the *Oxley* and *Otway* for the RAN, had their engines redesigned with increased bore and stroke to give 3,000 bhp and a surface speed of 15 knots.

The Os were 275 ft long, with a beam of 27.75 ft and carried a crew of 50. They were also the first British submarines to carry two 21-inch stern tubes, to complement the powerful bow armament of 6 tubes. Allied to this they had a greater diving depth and endurance, and a very much improved radio transmitter. The days of 'bird messengers' were gone for good. A 4-inch gun was fitted and they carried 16 torpedoes. They displaced 1,598 ton surfaced and 1,872 ton submerged. Most of them went to the China Station and served there until recalled to the Mediterranean during the war, where their losses were high. Their introduction into the Command was also the first

The *Rorqual* (above) was the only one of the class to survive the war, during which her mines sank at least two 4,000-ton merchant ships and two torpedo boats. She torpedoed a 3,000-ton vessel. The balloon or pressure-tight tanks were built into the forward structure to balance the mines aft. She was taken out of service in April 1946.

time that names were used instead of the more familiar class numbers.

Of similar design and armament but with a flared bow and larger conning-tower were the P and R Classes, ordered in the 1927 and 1928 programmes. These large ocean-going submarines were 287 ft long, with a beam of 30 ft, and were armed with six 21-inch bow and two stern 21-inch torpedo tubes. A powerful twin 2,200-hp diesel combination drove them at 17.5 knots surfaced and a standard 1,320-hp electric motor gave them 9 knots submerged. To give some idea of endurance, the *Regulus* for instance, started a 28-day patrol exercise on 5 January 1938, and completed 3,940 miles on the surface and 390 miles submerged. They had a crew of 50 and were named: *Parthian, Pandora, Perseus, Poseidon, Proteus* and *Phoenix*; *Rainbow, Regent, Regulus* and *Rover*.

The Porpoise Class was Britain's first class of purpose-built minelayers but when torpedo tubes were eventually used for minelaying, the need for this specialized type of submarine

HM Submarine *Subtle*.

disappeared. These powerful boats were 289 ft long and displaced 2,140 ton submerged. They carried a crew of 55 and were armed with six 21-inch torpedo tubes and a 4-inch gun. They were estimated to have cost £350,000 each.

They were layers of the spherical horned contact type of mine, with a mine casing high enough for a man to walk upright inside it. Two mining rails like tram-lines stretched the entire length of the casing and on these were the 'train' of 50 mines. The casing had large stern doors opened by remote control. The mines and sinkers sank to the bottom. A soluble plug in the sinker then let the mine rise on a cable to the pre-set depth. The submarines were named: *Porpoise, Narwhal, Rorqual, Grampus, Cachalot* and *Seal*.

The Shark Class was another attempt to improve on the L design and was a much smaller type of overseas patrol submarine. Built to the highest standards and incorporating the latest technology, they came into service from 1934 onwards. The first were named: *Sturgeon, Starfish, Shark, Swordfish, Sealion, Seahorse, Seawolf, Sunfish, Salmon, Snapper, Spearfish* and *Sterlet*. During the massive re-armament programme from 1936 onwards, additional S-boats were ordered. A total of 62 were built, more than for any previous class in the Navy.

The S Class *Seneschal* (top) and *Scythian*.

Proved in the North Sea's turbulent conditions, the first were: *Safari, Sahib, Saracen, Sceptre* and *Satyr*. The rest were to be 9 ft longer and were named: *Sibyl, Sea Dog, Sea Rover, Sea Nymph, Seraph, Shakespeare, Sickle, Simoon, Sirdar, Sportsman, Splendid, Spiteful, Stoic, Stonehenge, Storm, Stratagem, Strongbow, Scythian, Stubborn, Surf, Spark, Syrtis, Shalimar, Sea Devil, Spirit, Statesman, Scotsman, Sturdy, Stygian, Subtle, Supreme, Selene, Seneschal, Sea Scout, Sentinel, Scorcher, Saga, Sidon, Sleuth, Spearhead, Solent, Springer, Spur, Sanguine* and *P222*.

They displaced a mere 960 ton submerged, carried an average crew of 40 and were armed with six 21-inch bow tubes (some of the later ones had one stern tube fitted), and carried 13 torpedoes. They cost approximately £245,000. This was the first of two standardized types, the other being the much larger T Class with a planned 42-day patrol endurance. Reliability was a key factor in the design with everything made as simple as possible, and the designed diving depth was 300 ft, although many were to dive far beyond it. There were 22 of the class ordered in the 1935–7 programmes and commissioned between 1937 and 1939. They were named the Triton Class – after the first of the class and were: *Triton, Thetis, Tribune, Trident, Taku, Tarpon, Thistle, Triumph, Triad, Tigris, Talisman, Truant, Tuna, Tetrarch, Torbay, Traveller, Tempest, Thorn, Thrasher, Trooper, Trusty* and *Turbulent.* Powerfully armed with eight 21-inch bow external tubes and two forward on deck, they were to write epic chapters in the history of the Command.

Following the outbreak of war, a further batch was ordered and delivered, they were: *P311, Turpin, Thermopylae, Tasman, Teredo, Tactician, Thule, Tireless, Taurus, Templar, Token, Trespasser, Truculent, Talent, Tudor, Tarn, Tapir, Taciturn, Tabard, Truncheon, Trump, Trenchant, Tradewind, Tally-Ho, Thorough, Telemachus, Totem, Tiptoe, Tantivy, Terrapin* and *Tantalus.*

The first batch with riveted hulls had the two deck tubes mounted either side of the conning-tower, angled outwards at seven and a half degrees. The torpedoes were fitted with a compensation device so that after firing, they ran dead ahead.

In another batch these tubes were removed and were replaced with two or three stern tubes, while the bow tubes had two added in a special casing. During the war years, many of the class had up to five external tubes which could not be reloaded at sea. They carried 16 torpedoes and were armed with a 4-inch gun, and their endurance was increased from 6,900 to 11,000 miles by the conversion of Nos 3 and 5 ballast tanks to carry fuel.

After the war ended, those remaining were to be modernized, but the riveted hulls of some proved a disadvantage and only five were streamlined. These, were also refitted with six bow tubes only, and given a modern sonar and a fin-type conning-tower. They were *Tapir, Tireless, Talent, Teredo* and *Token.*

Between 1950 and 1956, eight of the welded-hull type were completely rebuilt, with hulls cut in two and lengthened. Improved diesel–electric propulsion was fitted giving a submerged speed of 15 knots maximum. Modern noise reduction techniques were incorporated, new sensors were added, and they were streamlined and given a fin-type conning-tower. The eight were: *Tabard, Trump, Truncheon, Tiptoe, Taciturn, Thermopylae, Totem* and *Turpin.*

The submarine had to operate on its own, in an eerie and often desolate world beneath the sea, totally dependent on its own resources, able to receive messages but unable to transmit them – a strange and

The *Tally-Ho* (above) which torpedoed the Japanese light cruiser *Kuma* in 1945, and a photograph of the modernized *Truncheon* (below).

frightening world in which to live and fight. In a T Class for example, the pressure hull was only 260 ft long and 16 ft in diameter, and in this thin steel tube, in tropical waters, the temperature in the engine room could rise to above 90 degrees, and it was not unusual for them to collect over 40 gallons of water from condensation in any one 24-hour period.

A steel catwalk ran the entire length of the boat and was full of holes like a colander, to minimize resistance to the sea when submerging. The bridge and gun casing were not armoured and were free-flooding, and the only access to them was through the lower and upper hatches in the conning-tower. Quite a lot of the metal was brass to avoid magnetic interference with the compass. On either side of the pressure hull were the main ballast tanks which filled completely when submerging, and there were trimming tanks throughout the entire length of the submarine. Compressed air could be forced in to drive out the water when the submarine wanted to surface.

The enormous electric batteries were each of 336 cells weighing half a ton each, and could be used in series for slow speed and long endurance, or in parallel for short bursts at high speed to get into an attacking position. Some five tons of distilled water was needed to top up the batteries. A 'snort' mast, some 14-inch in diameter, sucked air in to the diesel engines and had a 'float' valve over the open end to stop water entering should the sea break over the top of the inlet. The snort induction took the gases from the engines to the outside, just below sea level. These were not fitted until after the war.

In a submerged submarine, the crew can breathe the same air for a number of hours. Normal air contains some 78 per cent nitrogen, 21 per cent oxygen and minute traces of carbon dioxide. Normal exhaled air consists of 80 per cent nitrogen, 16 per cent oxygen and about 4 per cent carbon dioxide. Long after it became impossible to light a match through lack of oxygen, a human could still work and think. After 15 hours there could be stress, and after 24 hours each human would virtually be surrounded by a 'halo' of foul air. Chemical canisters could absorb the carbon dioxide and oxygen candles could – to a certain extent – replace the lack of oxygen. The most dangerous gas was hydrogen, discharged when an electric battery was charging or discharging. The most careful ventilation was often insufficient to prevent small pockets of the gas collecting in corners, where a tiny spark or a lighted match could cause a disastrous explosion.

By 1944, the wartime torpedo was 22 ft long, 21-inch in diameter and cost £2,500. External tubes where fitted could not be reloaded. Fired by compressed air, it could average about 45 knots for five miles, and normal safety precautions caused it to sink at the end of its run if it failed to hit the target. It weighed some 3,600 lb, and firing it meant that immediate adjustments were needed to maintain the submarine's trim. The torpedo was loaded through the rear door, which was then shut, and the portion not taken up by the torpedo was flooded by an internal tank, so that the 'front door' could be opened to the sea for firing. On firing, the submarine was lighter, but sea-water rushing into the tube checked the tendency to rise and automatic flooding of internal ballast tanks quickly regained the trim and allowed the submarine to remain on an even keel. After firing, the door open to the sea was shut, and the tube drained of water before reloading.

The bridge, built up from the casing, contained a chart table, watertight compass, engine-room telegraph and the usual voice pipe – the lid of which had to be slammed shut when diving – to the control room. From the bows, up to the two periscope standards, and down to the stern, ran a heavy 'jump-wire', to help protect the submarine from underwater mine mooring-wires and sweep-wires from surface warships.

There was no air-conditioning and the escape hatches were often fastened down – they operated at depths where the Davis escape apparatus would be useless and the hatches had been known to open under depth-charge attacks. The control room contained the heavy bronze tubes of the binocular search, and monocular attack, periscopes. These rested in heavy metal 'sheaths' which supported them when raised. The search periscope produced two images, the fainter one was adjusted until it appeared exactly over a portion of the enemy warship the height of which was exactly known. The Captain would state: 'Range is that,' and the man behind him would read off the inclination between the two lenses. A slide rule gave the range. Next order would be: 'Bearing is that,' which was read off a scale on the periscope to give the angle of attack.

Twelve mines of the magnetic Mk 2 variety could be carried and were loaded one at a time in the internal tubes. Expelled by compressed air, they planed gently to the bottom guided by a fin, but as the submarine also passed over them, she had to be efficiently degaussed – protected from her own magnetic field which could set the mine off. The mine reached the seabed and a soluble plug in the sinker then released a set length of cable. The mine rose to this set depth ready to trap the unwary.

During 1928, after the K Class submarines had been removed from the active list, Rear-Admiral Submarines declared an interest in submarines which, in an ocean war, would be capable of operating

View from forward of the starboard engine of the *Thames*.

with the Fleet. Although there were no diesel engines at that time capable of driving submarines as fast as surface craft, the Admiralty still held to the Fleet-submarine concept and the River Class design was submitted to the Board in June 1929.

HMS *Thames* – the first of the class – *Severn* and *Clyde* were quite conventional in design without huge guns or other unusual features. These first three of a projected class of 20 submarines were all built by Vickers at Barrow and were part double-hulled and well streamlined. Costing just over £500,000 each they were large and comfortable, but to keep down weight the diving depth was reduced from the 500 ft of the *Odin* to 300 ft by reducing the thickness of the pressure-hull plating from 35 to 25 lb per square inch.

The Admiralty-designed diesels were huge 10-cylinder engines developing a total of 8,000 hp at 400 rpm. The two vertical four-stroke blast injection engines weighed 347 ton. The engines could be supercharged by using two auxiliary generators driven by Ricardo sleeve-valve engines, to give a total of 10,000 hp.

The *Thames* when surfacing, experienced heavy listing due to a water build up in the main tanks on one side and this problem was overcome by modifying the position of the flooding holes. Due to her size, she also rolled heavily when surfacing 'beam on' in heavy seas and

91

HM Submarine *Severn*.

subsequently, whenever possible, she was surfaced head-on to rough seas. As in the overseas types, the Thames Class carried oil fuel in external tanks but these tanks, instead of being riveted as in the overseas types, were of all-welded construction.

With the stern tube removed, torpedo armament was six 21-inch bow tubes with 12 torpedoes carried. There was a 4.7-inch gun which was later changed to a 4-inch quick firer with 120 rounds of ammunition. With a length overall of 345 ft, they had a beam of 28.25 ft and the pressure hull had a depth of 18.25 ft. They displaced 1,805 ton on the surface and 2,860 ton submerged. Twin shafts drove the *Thames* to a record surface speed for the day of 21.5 knots. Surface endurance was given as 10,000 miles at 8 knots and 118 miles at 4 knots submerged. For short high-speed bursts she could manage 13 miles at 10 knots submerged. The crew totalled 61 officers and men.

A change in Admiralty policy during 1933 saw the remainder of the class cancelled. The three already built served during the Second World War although misemployed in the North Sea and Mediterranean. *Clyde* took part in the vital 'cargo bus' supply to Malta in September 1941, when she carried 1,200 ton of stores. Although successful as a class, they were no more so than submarines costing half as much to build. The *Thames* was lost off Norway on 2–3 August

92

HMS *Upstart*.

1940 – probably mined. The *Severn* and *Clyde* were taken off the active
service list while in the Far East in April and October 1945
respectively.

At the same time as these submarines were being built, 12 small
patrol-type submarines were ordered in February 1928 from Chatham,
Cammell Laird and Scotts. Named the Swordfish and Shark Classes,
they were based on the saddle-tank design of the L Class and were the
forerunners of the famous S Class that served with distinction during
the Second World War.

There remains one more important class which was, with the S and
T Classes, to bear the brunt of the war. This was the Unity Class
ordered under the 1936 programme probably as a replacement for the
obsolete H Class, nearly all of which had gone to the scrap heap. It was
to be the standard coastal patrol training submarine for the Royal Navy
and was to prove itself superbly throughout the Second World War.

The first three commissioned just before the war were: *Undine*,
Unity and *Ursula*, with four bow tubes. Another 53 were ordered but
only 34 were completed: *Una, Umpire, Undaunted, Union, Urchin* and
Urge, Unbeaten, Unique, Upholder, Upright, Usk and *Utmost*. In late
1940 with a redesigned bow to give a finer entry into the water, another
batch (some with numbers) was added: *P32, 33, 36, 38, 39, 48* and *82*
(later named *Upshot*); *Ultimatum, Uproar, Umbra, Unbending*,

The V Class submarines of the Second World War were designed 1935–6 and began to enter service in 1938. They served on coastal patrols in the Mediterranean and the Baltic. This is HM Submarine *Upshot*, completed 1944 and scrapped at Preston 1949.

Escape practice in harbour using the Davis Submarine Escape Apparatus, with splinter-proof glasses for eye protection.

Unbroken, Unseen, Unison, United, Unrivalled, Unshaken, Unsparing, Universal, Usurper, Untamed, Untiring, Uther, Unswerving and *Upstart*. Others were built for the Polish and for the Royal Netherlands Navy.

Submarine disasters, with their heavy loss of life, led to many ingenious devices for saving the lives of trapped submariners, but most of them were too heavy and took up too much space – always at a premium in an operational submarine.

One which was successful was developed by Mr Davis of Siebe Gorman, the diving experts, who had been working on the problem during the early 1920s. A major problem in escaping from a submarine at depth is the quick release of pressure on the body as it rises to the surface. Nitrogen is forced into the bloodstream and forms bubbles in the blood causing death by paralysis – the dreaded 'bends'. However, only oxygen is needed to survive, and this was the beauty of the Davis Submarine Escape Apparatus (DSEA).

It was simply an oxygen supply strapped to the chest, with an attached mask or 'second lung', through which the submariner could breath pure oxygen on his way up to the surface. Every submariner was trained in using the DSEA apparatus with the aid of special escape tanks, at the bottom of which were replicas of the air locks and escape chambers fitted in submarines.

The most famous escape using the apparatus was that of Petty Officer Willis from the *Poseidon* on 9 June 1931, after the submarine had collided with a Chinese steamer north of Wei-Hei-Wei. The majority of the crew escaped via the conning-tower before the *Poseidon* sank in 120 ft of water.

In the forepart of the submarine 24 men were trapped. All watertight doors were shut and DSEAs donned. The submarine was then flooded, but this took two hours ten minutes – there were no rapid-flood techniques as there are today. Oxygen supplies were running low. The hatch was opened as pressures equalized and two crew shot to the surface. One was dead. Pressure was again built up and four men escaped. The remainder died.

Later designs included special escape chambers built into the design, so that the lengthy flooding of the whole compartment could be avoided.

Current techniques use specially designed escape suits, fed with compressed air via a bleed valve, for 'free escape' breathing normal air. These enabled naval teams to make record escapes from the *Osiris*, 600 ft down during trials in the Mediterranean.

This dramatic picture was taken as a member of the diving team, led by Lieutenant-Commander Mathew Todd, made the record-breaking escape from 600 ft. Buoyancy in the suit shoots him high out of the water before falling back to float on the surface. The team worked out of Valletta Harbour.

4
SECOND WORLD WAR

Following the 1938 crisis, reservists were called up progressively from 15 June 1939 and all the submarines fit for operational service were manned. By August, Rear-Admiral Submarines, C. B. Watson, DSO, had moved the submarines and their depot ships to war stations.

HMS *Forth* and the 2nd Flotilla of eight S Class, three Ts and *Oxley*, moved to Dundee. The *Thames* was in refit.

The 6th Flotilla of three U Class, two Ls and the old *H32*, moved with the depot ship HMS *Titania* to Blyth. The 5th Flotilla, eight Hs and *Oberon* were in Portsmouth for training. There were just 21 operational submarines in Home waters and five of them were over ten years old. Four more of the S Class from Malta were based at Harwich with the old depot ship *Cyclops* as a foundation for the 3rd Flotilla, and the minelayer *Narwhal* – off station at home – was joined by the *Cachalot* and *Porpoise*.

Gibraltar had the *Clyde* and *Severn*, and the minelayer *Seal* was on passage to the China Station where the powerful 4th Flotilla was based, totalling 15 submarines. At Malta was a varied collection of three minelayers, four S Class, two Os and the *Otway*. On 31 August at 16.00, all the submarines sailed for prepared positions on patrol, and the signal to commence hostilities was sent at 11.00 on 3 September 1939.

Under the 1937 Estimates, seven of the T Class were due to be completed in 1939, three were to be completed in 1940 and one in 1941. The Emergency War Programme gave orders for seven T Class and twelve U Class.

H Boats in harbour and (right) crews boarding L Class submarines.

As early as 5 September 1938, Rear-Admiral Submarines had suggested moving his headquarters staff from Fort Blockhouse to Rosyth, which was proposed as the Home Fleet's operational base. No suitable facilities were available at Rosyth and eventually after extensive alterations had been completed, most of the staff moved to Corriemar House, Aberdour, near Rosyth, on 30 August 1939. The administrative staff stayed at Fort Blockhouse.

The Command was a peculiar one. Rear-Admiral Submarines was only responsible for administration, liaison and training. Operational control of the submarines came under the Flag Officer of the Fleet or the Senior Officer of the area to which they were attached. All this however changed in August 1938 when the Home Fleet Orders were revised and the Admiral assumed operational responsibility for all Home Command submarines. It also became obvious early on in the war that neither Dundee or Blyth could be protected against air attacks, and the 2nd Flotilla moved to Rosyth, with the *Forth* moving up on 14 October.

The submarine war opened with a disaster. The North Sea, where even on a fine day visibility rarely exceeds five miles and is more often only a mile, can be misty, or foggy with heavy cloud cover, and the seabed is uneven making navigation by soundings difficult. Accurate navigation is of supreme importance to all submarines but more particularly so when operating in wartime and in specified sectors. These designated areas were for protection against attack by British

aircraft or surface shipping, and bearing in mind the rudimentary state of recognition training, it was a matter of life or death for the submarine.

On 10 September 1939, the *Oxley* strayed from her patrol area in bad weather and was sighted by the *Triton* which fired a recognition grenade, but *Oxley* either didn't see it or her reply was faulty. *Triton* closed to an attacking position and torpedoed the *Oxley* which sank almost immediately. Only the Commanding Officer and a rating were saved.

It was not until 20 November that the *Sturgeon* (Lt G. D. A. Gregory) opened the British account by torpedoing a German anti-submarine trawler in the open waters of the Heligoland Bight. On 4 December the *Salmon* (Lt-Cdr E. O. Bickford) skilfully tracked and torpedoed the outward bound *U36* west of the Skaggerak, and on 13 December she fired a salvo at long range and scored hits on the German light cruisers *Nürnberg* and escort. The next day *Ursula* (Lt-Cdr G. C. Phillips), close in to Heligoland, torpedoed the light cruiser *Leipzig*. A torpedo which passed under the cruiser sank the torpedo boat *F9* and a gunboat. As a result, *Nürnberg* was out of the war for five months and *Leipzig* for a year, after which she was used as a training vessel. The rather disappointing results of the torpedo hits emphasized the watertight integrity of German cruisers. Both Bickford and Phillips were promoted to Commander and awarded the DSO.

The *Forth* at sea with some of her 'brood'.

With the White Ensign flying in the breeze, HM Submarine *Sturgeon*, which sank a 3,335-ton German transport off the coast of Denmark, returns to port.

HMS *Sturgeon* (640 ton) was launched at Chatham in 1932 and was commanded by Lt. G. D. A. Gregory, DSO, photographed here with his crew. Gregory is seen in the back row, fifth from left.

The bleak picture at the end of 1939 reflected the great disappointment felt throughout the Command at the results obtained so far. British submarines had sunk three small minor warships and one U-boat, and damaged two light cruisers. The *Oxley* had been lost, and *Triumph* had been badly damaged by a mine. Worse was to come. Between 6 and 9 January 1940, in or near Heligoland, Britain lost the *Undine*, *Seahorse* and *Starfish*. By contrast, the German U-boats had sunk the aircraft carrier *Courageous*, damaged the battleship *Barham*, and penetrated the Fleet anchorage at Scapa Flow to sink the battleship *Royal Oak*.

It must be remembered however that few of the home-based submarines had been trained for a wartime role. The major part of their peacetime exercises had been in acting as targets for the Navy's rapidly improving anti-submarine destroyers and smaller craft. The best trained crews were with the China Fleet operating submarines that were too big for the North Sea or the Mediterranean. There were far too few submarines for the commitments Britain had to meet.

Rear-Admiral Watson was promoted to Vice-Admiral and later appointed as Flag Officer Greenock. On 9 January 1940, Vice-Admiral Sir Max Horton was brought back as Vice-Admiral Submarines and his vast experience as a submariner was soon put to the test as the invasion of Norway became a threat. By March 1940, the Admiral decided to cover the exits from the Kattegat and Heligoland Bight, east of the German-declared mining area, and selected points along the Norwegian coast. Nineteen submarines were sailed including the famous Polish submarine *Orzel* which made a dramatic escape from the Germans to join the British forces.

Orzel opened the account on 8 April when she torpedoed and sank the 5,261 ton troop-ship *Rio de Janeiro* off Christiansund South, and

The Polish submarine *Orzel*.

the following day an Admiralty order to sink any transports was issued. On 11 April, authority was given to sink any ships within ten miles of the Norwegian coast. These orders gave the Command an unequalled opportunity to show their skill and daring. They re-established the greatness handed down to them by people like Nasmith and Horton himself, in a series of devastating attacks on the troop-ships, merchantmen and warships invading Norway.

There were some amazing escapes. *Tetrarch* (Lt-Cdr R. G. Mills) attacked a large merchantman and was forced under by heavy depth-charge attacks. She was unable to surface the next day because of daylight and remained submerged for a record 43 hours before escaping. Often reaching depths of 400 ft, the air was foul, the batteries nearly drained and oxygen was used to keep the crew going by relieving violent headaches and sickness. When she surfaced at 21.30 on 24 April, many of the crew got drunk on fresh air. It was reported that nobody went hungry and few of the crew ate anything for 30 hours.

The pocket battleship *Lützow* was attacked by the *Spearfish* (Lt J.

Seen below is the submarine depot ship HMS *Tyne*, with some of the submarines she was 'mothering' tied up alongside. Depot ships, whether custom-built or converted liners, played a vital part in keeping British submarines operational and providing comfortable accommodation for crews when resting between patrols.

Safely home after their hazardous duties at sea, a British submarine crew
going on board a depot ship for rest while their underwater craft is overhauled
by naval experts. Every comfort was provided for the submarine crews on
board the depot ship, including a large recreation room, private lockers and
hot baths.

The submarine slips down the estuary in the evening light. She goes alone, with few to watch her. Only the men of her depot ship and of the submarines still secured alongside were there to wonder how she would fare.

More than five hundred skilled naval craftsmen worked in the different departments on board a submarine depot ship. In this floating factory spare parts were carried for every replacement. Men are seen above repairing torpedoes in the workshops.

H. Forbes) with a salvo of six torpedoes. Hits blew off the propellers, made the steering gear useless and put her out of action for a year.

The *Sunfish* (Lt-Cdr J. E. Slaughter) rounded off one patrol by sinking four merchantmen of 7,000, 6,000, 3,000, and 2,500 ton. In the *Snapper*, Lt W. D. A. King sank a tanker by gunfire and destroyed two smaller craft. The *Truant* (Lt-Cdr C. H. Hutchinson) torpedoed and sank the cruiser *Karlsruhe*, and the submarine dived to over 300 ft and stayed there for three hours, to avoid heavy and continuous depth-charge attacks.

Britain had her losses. On 10 April the *Thistle* was torpedoed by *U4*, on 14 April *Tarpon* was sunk by the minesweeper *M6*, and on 18 April the *Sterlet* was sunk by three A/S vessels.

During the first phase of the campaign the British had sunk some 50,000 ton of merchant shipping; a German cruiser, two minesweepers, an anti-submarine corvette, and the *U1* which was mined. A battleship had been badly damaged. Britain had lost three submarines and the minelayer *Seal* was captured.

The unusual capture of a submarine by the Germans deserves an explanation. Lt-Cdr R. P. Lonsdale in the *Seal*, had laid a minefield in

Lieutenant W. D. King, wearing the light-coloured jacket, in the conning-tower of the S Class submarine *Snapper*, returning to harbour after the Norwegian patrol which gained him the DSO.

the Kattegat across the Germany–Norway sea lanes and was hunted by surface warships. The submarine picked up a trailing mine and three hours later, while still under attack, there was a heavy explosion outboard and *Seal* bottomed at 130 ft. Lonsdale remained on the bottom until dark and when the main ballast tanks were blown, the submarine took a steep angle upwards while the stern was held on the bottom by a flooded after compartment.

Any movement was difficult because of the steep angle, and on the afternoon of the following day the air was foul. Only six of the 54 crew attended prayers. Checking on the compressed air remaining, an air bottle was found in the engine room. This compressed air was fed to the after tanks and the submarine shot to the surface. One engine was started but the submarine only ran in circles because of the damaged stern and came under attack by seaplanes. Desperate attempts to fight back were halted when the Lewis gun jammed and a trawler arrived on the scene. Believing the badly damaged submarine would sink, the crew abandoned it and surrendered. *Seal* remained afloat, however, and was towed by the jubilant Germans to a Danish port under their control.

With the fall of France in June 1940, the Portsmouth submarines had to extend their patrols to cover the Channel ports and those of the French Biscay. British forces were augmented by the arrival of the large French submarine *Surcouf* and six smaller ones, and most of the crews agreed to remain with the British and work under Admiral Horton.

On 20 June, the *Clyde* (Lt-Cdr D. C. Ingram) torpedoed the *Gneisenau* off the Norwegian coast and put her out of action for many months. In the first of many successful undercover operations, the *Seawolf* (Lt-Cdr J. W. Studholme) landed two Norwegian officers on Ullers Island and took them off four days later.

On 5 July, the *Shark* (Lt P. N. Buckley) reported that she was unable to dive. The submarine fought a five-hour duel with flying boats using depth-charges for the first time, and was heavily machine-gunned. The *Shark* was scuttled and the crew taken prisoner. July was disastrous. On 14 July, *Salmon* failed to return from a patrol; on 22 July, *Narwhal* disappeared while laying mines off Trondheim, and the *Thames* left Dundee on patrol and was not heard of again. On 1 August, the *Spearfish* was sunk, and in the October, the old *H49* was sunk off the Dutch coast.

One of the S-boats, the *Stubborn* commanded by Lieutenant A. A. Duff, was patrolling off Trondheim in February 1944 and had already sunk 4,000 ton of shipping, when she attacked another convoy

Companionship in danger makes up for the discomfort of the working spaces in the diesel-engine room (above) and the mess deck or living quarters (below).

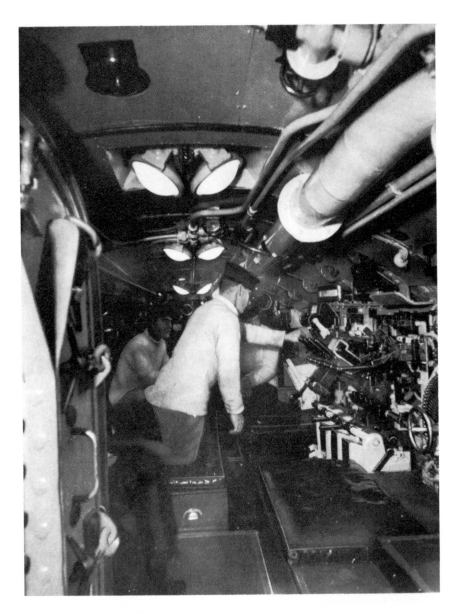

Seen above are crewmen controlling the main electric motors of a submarine submerged during a wartime patrol. Top right: the fore ends of a submarine with torpedoes in their tubes and spares in their racks, and below: the attack team closed up with a Chief Petty Officer and a rating controlling the hydroplanes.

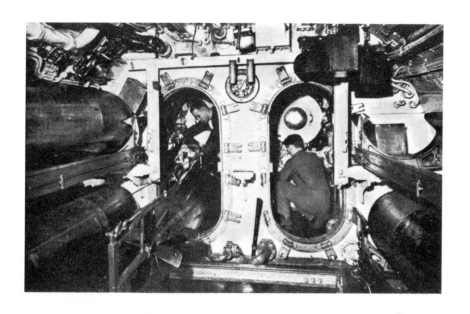

Cheer ship! HM Submarine *Sunfish* commanded by Lt-Cdr J. Slaughter, DSO, returning to harbour from Norway after sinking four enemy ships.

unsuccessfully and was heavily and accurately depth-charged. The after hydroplane jammed in the dive position and the submarine plunged to a depth of some 400 ft, before the main ballast tanks were blown.

She shot to the surface and burst out of the water in sight of the enemy, but just as suddenly dived again, this time reaching the enormous depth of 500 ft. The enemy continued to depth-charge which put the ASDIC set out of action, to add to the damaged rudder and internal ballast tank suffered in the earlier attacks. The depth-charges were set too shallow and although it was known by 1943 that some German U-boats operated at 600 ft, the enemy probably believed no British submarine could reach that depth.

More than seven hours later, *Stubborn* surfaced – with an estimated seventy-degree bow-up angle – and came out of the water like a rocket. Despite the damage, and later the rudder broke down completely, the submarine made her way back over 300 miles on the surface, and was eventually towed into Lerwick.

The first submarine ever to give passage to a woman was the *Truant*

(Lt-Cdr H. A. V. Haggard) when the vessel was *en route* from America to Gibraltar. The Norwegian motor vessel *Tropic Sea* was sighted heading for Bordeaux and the *Truant* closed her with gun manned and ordered her to stop, not to use her wireless and to send a boat over with the Captain and ship's papers. A large number of men began to abandon ship and *Truant* moved in among the boats to find the Captain.

When found he was the German Captain of a prize crew taking the ship, its prisoners and 8,000 ton of wheat to France. Lt-Cdr Haggard also found the Captain and his wife and 22 other survivors from the British S.S. *Saxby*. The *Tropic Sea* was blown apart by scuttling charges set by the Germans and the *Saxby*'s crew including the lady, continued to Gibraltar in the *Truant*.

Perhaps the supreme achievement of Submarine Command was the campaign in the Mediterranean, which began with 17 submarines of the O and P Classes and similar R Class. The large, ocean-going submarines should never have operated in the Mediterranean at all. Its coastal shallows, transparent waters and frequent calms were more suited to small patrol submarines like the Rs and later, the U Class.

As diplomatic relations with Italy worsened, all British submarines east of Suez, including the 4th Flotilla from Singapore and the 8th from Colombo, were sailed for Alexandria to form the 1st Flotilla. Six submarines stayed at Alexandria with the depot ship *Medway*, and the other six went to Malta. During the first two weeks after Italy declared war on 10 June 1940, Britain lost the *Grampus* (Lt-Cdr C. A. Rowe) which failed to return from a minelaying patrol off Port Augusta on 13 June. On 26 June, *Odin* (Lt-Cdr K. M. Woods) and *Orpheus* (Lt-Cdr J. A. S. Wise) were lost. Half the Malta force had been wiped out.

On 31 July, *Phoenix* (Lt-Cdr G. N. Nowell) was lost and *Oswald* (Lt-Cdr D. A. Fraser) was sunk by an Italian destroyer in the Straits of Messina. Yet, by February 1941, the submarines from Alexandria and the newly formed 10th Flotilla from Malta – now including some of the U Class – had sunk some 300,000 ton of enemy shipping. At the end of two years war in the Mediterranean, 500,000 ton including 70 supply ships and six troop-carrying liners had been sunk. But, Britain had also lost 70 officers, 720 ratings – highly skilled crews who were irreplaceable in a wartime situation – and 14 submarines.

The first submarine VC of this war was awarded to Lieutenant-Commander M. D. Wanklyn, DSO, 'for valour and resolution in command of H.M. Submarine *Upholder*'. On 24 May he was patrolling off the coast of Sicily when a southbound enemy troop convoy was sighted with a strong destroyer escort. Despite the fact that the submarine's listening gear was out of action and fading light made periscope observation difficult, the sea conditions made a surface attack impossible. Wanklyn pressed home his attack with great daring and closed the convoy to short range. He just avoided being rammed by a destroyer but brought his sights on and torpedoed the 18,000-ton liner *Conte Rosso*, carrying troop reinforcements for North Africa. During the next 20 minutes the submarine survived repeated attacks during which 37 depth-charges were dropped.

Before this attack, he had been awarded the DSO after sinking a tanker and a merchant ship. In September 1941 he torpedoed and sank two 19,500-ton liners the *Neptunia* and *Oceania*, even despite a gyrocompass failure. He had to close at full speed on the surface using the magnetic compass, and by anticipating the amount of swing, fired the salvo by eye alone. The *Upholder* failed to return from patrol on 18 April 1943, but by this time Wanklyn had sunk two U-boats, an 1,800-ton destroyer and at least 97,000 ton of merchant shipping.

In announcing the loss of *Upholder* on 22 August 1942, the Board of Admiralty's communiqué said unusually: 'It is seldom proper for Their Lordships to draw distinction between different services rendered in the course of naval duty, but they take this opportunity of singling out those of HMS *Upholder*, under the command of Lieutenant-Commander Wanklyn, for special mention.

'She was long employed against enemy communications in the Central Mediterranean in that arduous and dangerous duty. Such was the standard of skill and daring set by Lieutenant-Commander Wanklyn and the officers and men under him, that they and their ship became an inspiration not only to their own flotilla, but to the Fleet of which it was a part and to Malta, where for so long *Upholder* was based. The ship and her company are gone, but the example and inspiration remain.'

Another 'classic' escape from disaster involved the submarine *Thrasher* commanded by Lt Hugh Mackenzie, known to his intimates as 'Red Rufus' (later Vice-Admiral Sir Hugh, KCB DSO DSC, Chief Polaris Executive). A heavily escorted supply ship was sunk off Suda Bay in 1942. During a heavy counter-attack by surface ships and aircraft, 33 depth-charges were dropped but when *Thrasher* surfaced at night, two unexploded aircraft bombs were found in the forward casing in almost inaccessible positions. The submarine was still close to the enemy coast and in an area where surface warships could be expected constantly. The First Lieutenant, P. S. Roberts, and Petty Officer T. W. Gould volunteered for the dangerous task of removing the bombs. Apart from the ordinary dangers of bomb disposal, they

Winners of the Victoria
Cross. Lieutenant P. S.
Roberts (top left), Petty
Officer T. W. Gould (above)
and Lieutenant-Commander
M. D. Wanklyn, DSO.

would almost certainly be drowned if the submarine had to dive suddenly.

They crawled through the low casing on their stomachs and easily disposed of the first bomb, which was lying on the casing. The second one was inside it and the two men, one pushing and one pulling, had to move it over 20 feet, until it could be hoisted out and cleared. The whole operation was carried out by the faint light from a shielded torch. The bomb was about three feet six inches long and every time it was moved there was a loud screeching noise. The operation took a breathtaking 50 minutes before Roberts was able to put it in a sack and lower it overboard. Both men were awarded the VC.

Lazaretto was the name of the famous Malta base on Manoel Island, between the Sliema and Marsa Muscetto creeks, north-west of Grand Harbour. During the first phase of the heavy air-raids when repairs could not be done ashore, submarines coming in from patrol handed over to a spare crew. They took the submarine out to sea in daylight hours and lay on the bottom while the first crew rested as best they could ashore. The submarine surfaced at night so that repairs could be caried out.

When the Russian campaign started, there was a lull in the attacks on the island, during which time, underground workshops and safe sleeping accommodation was built underground.

Operations from Malta were only made possible by the 'Magic Carpet Service' provided by the minelayers and other large submarines operating out of Alexandria, carrying supplies to the base. The minelayer *Porpoise* started the 'service' carrying petrol and mines and as a bonus, laid a minefield during the voyage. She made a total of nine trips to Malta as an underwater freighter. During July 1941 alone, the 'service' carried 126 passengers, 84,280 gallons of petrol, 83,340 gallons of kerosene, 12 ton of mail, 30 ton of stores and six ton of ammunition including torpedoes. The submarines continued operations although the base was hit by an estimated 400 bombs during 1,000 raids.

However, despite the heavy air attacks and the lack of spares and torpedoes restricting operations, the submarines operating in the Mediterranean were a constant threat to the Axis powers as ship after ship, carrying oil, petrol, aviation spirit, stores and troops, were sent to the bottom. Between Italy's entry into the war and her surrender on 11 September 1943 the submarines sank 1,335,000 ton of shipping.

Among the early reinforcements sent to the Mediterranean from Home waters were Commander J. W. 'Tubby' Linton in *Pandora* and then in *Turbulent* and Commander Anthony Miers in *Torbay*.

Even in the island's blackest days submarines still sailed from Malta to attack the enemy's North Africa supply lines.

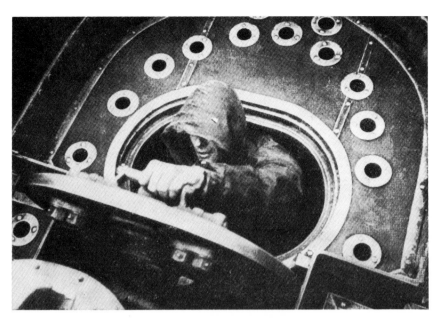

The Captain climbs through the conning-tower hatch as the submarine surfaces. The metal-rimmed holes drain away the sea-water.

Commander Linton's 'bag' was to include a cruiser, a destroyer, a U-boat and 28 supply ships, totalling nearly 100,000 ton. He was eventually lost when the *Turbulent* was sunk by depth-charges off the coast of Corsica, but was awarded a posthumous VC to add to the DSO and DSC he had already won.

Commander Miers (later Rear-Admiral Sir Anthony, VC KBE CB DSO), was another great submariner cast in much the same mould. A typical patrol while in command of the *Torbay* was that of 4 March 1942 when the submarine was dived to avoid being rammed by a destroyer. The upper conning-tower hatch jammed but just in time the lower hatch was clipped and fastened. The conning-tower flooded and with all electrical circuits shorted, the klaxon and diving alarms blared forth until the fuses could be withdrawn. Unable to get into an attacking position on a troop convoy that passed by unmolested, Miers decided to follow it in to Corfu Harbour in the hopes of attacking when unloading began. Both north and south channels were narrow, but after charging batteries the *Torbay* penetrated the defences and entered Corfu Roads. To Miers' disappointment, he only found two supply ships which he attacked. On 5 March, the *Torbay* withdrew seawards after spending 17 hours inside the enemy harbour.

118

Commander Anthony Miers, VC DSO.

On 19 January 1942, HMS *Splendid* was launched. She displaced a modest 990 ton submerged but was to become famous under the command of Lieutenant I. L. M. McGeoch. Armed with seven 21-inch torpedo tubes, six bow and one stern, she was powered by a Vickers diesel–electric combination giving a speed of 14.75 knots surfaced and 9 knots submerged. Diving depth was quoted as 350 ft and the normal time for a dive was 25–30 seconds.

Commissioned as *P228* and built at Chatham Dockyard, she was named *Splendid* on 31 January 1943. She was the first British submarine to mount an Oerlikon anti-aircraft gun. On 21 April 1943, the *Splendid* was lost in action but five officers and 25 ratings were taken prisoner. She had sunk 38,771 ton of enemy warships and

HM Submarine *Tally-Ho* at sea on passage to the Far East and below: loading a 4-inch gun.

Pictured in dry dock, the gashes torn in the *Tally-Ho's* sides by the Japanese torpedo boat, and below: the business end of the *Tally-Ho* with her torpedo tubes which ended many a 'chase'.

merchant ships carrying vital petrol and stores for Rommel's forces. Her young Lieutenant became Vice-Admiral Sir Ian, KCB DSO DSC.

On 5 October 1979, Lady Anne Eberle, launched and named HMS *Splendid*, the sixth and last submarine of the Swiftsure Class of nuclear-powered hunter killers.

Towards the end of the war, the 10th Flotilla was still operating out of Malta and one of their youngest commanding officers was Lieutenant John Roxburgh, first in the *United* and then in *Tapir*. Between August and September 1943, he sank over 8,000 ton of enemy shipping.

Another submarine 'ace' was Lieutenant-Commander L. A. W. Bennington, DSO DSC, who had a tremendous record in the Mediterranean and then in the Far East where, in command of the *Tally-Ho*, he had one of the most remarkable encounters of the war. He torpedoed and sank the *UIT23* of 1,100 ton, the former Italian *Reginaldo Giuliani*, and was heavily engaged by the enemy. Later on in the patrol he met a Japanese torpedo boat head-on. They passed on opposite sides, so close that the torpedo boat's screws tore huge slanting gashes through the light plating of the port ballast tank. Despite the heavy damage, the *Tally-Ho* crept back through heavily patrolled enemy waters to reach Ceylon, 1,200 miles away. Bennington was back in action only ten weeks later to sink a further 13 junks, a 300-ton ship, and a Japanese sub-chaser in a gun duel.

On 2 December 1944, the *Tally-Ho* sailed from Trincomalee for home, some 13 months after her first patrol, having completed some 46,000 miles on her main engines at an average speed of 12 knots. She was placed on the disposal list in 1961 and sold for scrap on 23 February 1967.

In September 1944, Rear-Admiral C. B. Barry, DSO, became ill and was relieved on 12 September 1944 by Rear-Admiral G. E. Creasy, CB CBE DSO MVO, as Flag Officer Submarines. Britain had a force of nearly 40 submarines in the Far East and the USN Commander, Admiral King, considering this to be too many, proposed that some should operate out of Fremantle. This fell to the 8th Flotilla, later succeeded by the 4th. At Trincomalee, a new 2nd Flotilla was formed based on the depot ship HMS *Wolfe*, a converted liner. By 1945, the 4th Flotilla based on HMS *Adamant* was operating from Fremantle and the 8th Flotilla with HMS *Maidstone*, was at Subic Bay, Manilla.

In a book this size it is impossible to deal with the Far East in great detail, though during this period many British submarines did take part in clandestine operations, landing men, arms, ammunition and

Leading Seaman J.J. Magennis, VC.

supplies on enemy beaches, prior to the invasion of Malaya.

American success in destroying the bulk of Japanese merchant shipping made it difficult for the XE Class of midget submarines to find targets. On 31 July, *XE4* disrupted enemy communications when she cut the Singapore and Hong Kong cables to Saigon. On 31 July *XE1* (Lt J. E. Smart RNVR) and *XE3* (Lt I. E. Fraser RNR) were towed to the Horsburgh lighthouse before slipping their tows and entering the Johore Strait. There they found the Japanese heavy cruiser *Takao*, which was attacked and badly damaged by the team of Lieutenant Fraser and Leading Seaman J. J. Magennis. Only the fact that the cruiser was in shallow water prevented her being a complete loss. Both men were awarded the Victoria Cross.

On 7 June 1945, *Trenchant* (Cdr A. R. Hezlet, DSO DSC) moved north to cover the Australian landings at Brunei but was unable to get into position in time. She was authorized to carry out a reconnaissance of the Banka Strait, the narrow channel between Sumatra and Banka Island. A Dutch minefield blocked the main entrance and left a narrow 1.5-mile gap east of it. The *Trenchant* penetrated the channel and the following day sighted a Japanese heavy cruiser steaming at 15 knots and, blissfully unaware of the submarine, steering a straight course. Cdr Hezlet closed to within 3,000 yards and fired his massive salvo of eight bow tubes. Five hits were heard and despite valiant efforts to beach herself, the famous *Ashigara* of 13,000 ton, rolled over and sank. She was transporting thousands of troops to reinforce Singapore. This brilliant attack gained Hezlet his DSO and the United States Legion of Merit (Commander).

Earlier in 1945, the famous *Porpoise* (Lt-Cdr H. B. Turner) was lost. She was completing the laying of a second minefield off Penang, which she reported by radio. This elderly 'lady' carried her oil fuel in external tanks and it is thought that an oil slick, possibly due to an earlier heavy bombing attack, led to her destruction by Japanese anti-submarine vessels. She was the seventy-fourth and last British submarine lost in the Second World War.

A Celestial Being

As a prelude to the North African landings, three special operations were undertaken by the *Seraph* and the *Sybil*. On 19 October 1942, the *Seraph* (Lieutenant N. L. A. Jewell) left Gibraltar with Major-General Mark Clark and three other senior American Army officers on board.

The submarine reached the rendezvous point off the North African coast on 21 October and went to periscope depth. There was a light as arranged, shining from the window of a house on shore. Just before midnight a light flashed from the shore and the United States officers accompanied by three officers of the Commandos, landed from a collapsible dinghy. The submarine then retired and waited submerged throughout the following day. As night fell, instructions were received for the Lieutenant to bring his submarine as close inshore as he could, and he closed to some 400 yards with only a few feet of water under the keel.

Heavy seas pounding on the beach made it impossible for the collapsible boats to be launched and the submarine again withdrew, until the weather moderated early in the morning. The submarine was ordered to try again and *Seraph* was brought in as close as possible. The party safely boarded the submarine and the next day a Catalina flying boat landed nearby. The party were ferried to it and flew off, while the submarine returned to Gibraltar.

On 27 October *Seraph* sailed again, but this time for a rendezvous on the coast of France. On 5 October she reached the rendezvous, surfaced and allowed the current to drift the submarine slowly towards the land, with no engines to break the silence. With Lieutenant Jewell on the bridge, as they anxiously watched the shore, was Captain

HM Submarine *Seraph* whose clandestine operations were a prelude to the North African invasion.

Wright USN, nominally in command as the submarine was flying American colours. He had also been on the previous expedition.

After some hours, a small boat with muffled oars came alongside and the *Seraph* took on board the famous French General Giraud, his son and three others. The *Seraph* dived and made for her rendezvous with the flying boat which landed nearby and took the party off. It was 7 November – the day before the Allied landings in North Africa.

The last operation was by the *Sybil*, commanded by Lieutenant E. J. D. Turner, DSC, which sailed on 8 November for a rendezvous on the south coast of France. Moving slowly inshore, the submarine spent a couple of hours watching the headlights of cars and the lights of trains, moving along the coast. A small boat appeared and came alongside and a lady's voice was heard to say:

> *We seek him here, we seek him there,*
> *Those Frenchies seek him everywhere.*
> *Is he in heaven? – Is he in hell?*
> *That demmed elusive Pimpernel?*

Seven staff officers and officials of General Giraud climbed on board, including a lady, who remained in the submarine until the *Sybil* reached Algiers on 11 November.

These operations were typical of many carried out by British submarines world-wide during the course of the war.

Sink the Tirpitz

Of all the exciting operations and patrols carried out by Submarine Command during the war, the daring and audacity of the tiny X-craft when they crippled the German battleship *Tirpitz* most captured the imagination of the British people.

Admiral Six Max Horton was responsible for the development of this special submarine weapon, and the design in which the Admiralty first became interested was the work of Commander C. H. Varley, DSC, a submarine commander of the 1914–18 war. The prototype was launched in 1942 with trials and exhaustive tests carried out by Lieutenant W. G. Meeke, DSC. The officers and men were all volunteers for special and hazardous service. Training was in the charge of Captain T. I. S. Bell, DSC, and later Commander D. C. Ingram, DSC. The plans for the attack, code-named Source, were drawn up by Commander G. P. S. Davies of the Admiral's staff at Northways House. In April 1943, the Special Flotilla was formed under the command of Captain W. E. Banks, DSC.

These tiny craft, designed to cut though nets and attack capital ships which could not be brought to action in the open sea, were only 30 ton submerged, 51.25 ft long, with a beam of 5.75 ft – smaller by far than the original Holland Class. They were driven on the surface by a 42-hp diesel at some 6 knots, and submerged by a tiny 30-hp electric motor at 5 knots. They carried a crew of four, and after penetrating the well-defended enemy base they would release their two 2-ton charges under the hull. These would sink to the bottom where they would be exploded by a timing mechanism, the craft having retired.

On 11 September 1943, six X-craft left their base at Loch Cairnbawn, towed by their parent submarines, for the 1,000 mile journey to Norway. On 14 September, aerial pictures confirmed that *Tirpitz* and *Scharnhorst* were in Kaa Fjord and the *Lutzow* in Lange Fjord – both part of the Alten Fjord complex. The original plan was for *X5, 6,* and *7* to attack the *Tirpitz*; for *X9* and *10* the *Scharnhorst* and *X8* the *Lutzow*. The attack was planned for the night of 21/2 September. During the passage *X8* developed serious defects and was scuttled, and *X9*'s tow parted and she was lost.

On 20 September, the remainder with their operational crews on board left their parent submarines, and after passing though the minefields off Soroy Sound, waited in Alten Fjord to carry out the attack provisionally arranged for not before a minute past midnight, 00.01 GMT, on 22 September. In fact the COs had agreed to attack at

One of the X-craft on trials showing the accepted method of conning the midget submarine. Without a periscope, the CO rests his arms on a rail to which he was strapped.

first light. Then mechanical faults prevented *X10* carrying out her attack on the *Scharnhorst*. The others made the long passage of 60 miles up the fjord which was not only patrolled by surface craft, but also by listening posts, nets and gun defences. The *X5, 6,* and *7* breached the torpedo and anti-submarine nets round the *Tirpitz*, laid their charges and tried to retire. There was no escape, but a huge explosion so damaged the *Tirpitz* that she was no longer a fighting unit. One of the major menaces to the surface Fleet and merchant shipping taking supplies to Russia, had been removed.

Lieutenants B. C. G. Place, DSC and D. Cameron RNR, were subsequently awarded the VC. Lieutenant H. Henty-Creer RNVR and *X5* were lost. Place and Cameron scuttled their craft and together with the majority of their crews were taken prisoner. The citation for the awards read: 'the courage, endurance and utter contempt for danger in the immediate face of the enemy, shown by Lieutenants Cameron and Place during this determined and successful attack, were supreme'.

Lt Henty-Creer was only awarded a Mention in Despatches and for years his family tried to solve the mystery of what happened to the tiny *X5*.

In the late 1970s, a British diving expedition backed by the Imperial War Museum, the Winston Churchill Trust and industry, believed they had solved the mystery. It was known that one X-craft was scuttled beneath the *Tirpitz* and another was later taken ashore. The British Sub-Aqua Club's team of 16, found the bows of what they believed to be an X-craft upside down on the bottom of the fjord at 140 ft. Some 90 ft away was the midships section which had suffered severe damage to the plating, as if it had been pulled apart by sweep-wires which the Germans towed over the spot to find the strange craft. It had bobbed to the surface 400 yards off the starboard bow of the *Tirpitz* and come under severe fire from the secondary armament. It disappeared beneath the surface again, and the position had then been heavily depth-charged.

There was, however, no sign of the two giant 'saddle' mines or the cradles, and the wreck site was so close to the battleship's anchorage that experts reckon the *X5* did close its target – a feat discounted by Naval Intelligence at the time.

Rear-Admiral Godfrey Place, VC, one of the surviving captains, has said that he would have expected all the mines laid beneath the *Tirpitz* to have exploded together when the first timing mechanism was actuated. However, there is no way of ever finding out now how many mines did explode under the vessel and destroy her as a fighting ship.

Rear Admiral B. C. G. Place, VC DSC, in 1968.

The Sub-Aqua Club divers, unfortunately, did not stay long at the Kaa Fjord site. Whether the wreckage will ever be recovered or the truth of this mystery ever solved, remains to be seen.

These unique submersibles were followed by the slightly bigger XE Class, designed for operations in the Far East. They were flush-decked, had air-conditioning, a flooding chamber so that crew members could leave and return after attaching limpet mines to the hull of a warship, and were slightly bigger.

The other unique craft of the war were the electrically propelled two-man Chariots, which had a powerful bow charge in front of the machine, on which they sat externally. Their most important 'kills' were in the Mediterranean where they sank the Italian cruisers *Ulpio Traino* (3 January 1943), *Bolzano* (21 June 1944) and *Gorizia* (26 June 1944).

129

One of the two-man chariots is hoisted inboard after trials. The crew in diving suits, sat astride the torpedo which dived under the target before the explosive charge was fitted beneath the target.

XE8 casts off from HM Submarine *Subtle*. The two officers see their craft clear, calling orders down to the rest of the crew below.

Famous Survivors

On 31 December 1974, the oldest patrol submarine in the Royal Navy, HMS *Andrew* – then commanded by Lieutenant-Commander Paul Hoddinott – retired after an active service life of 26 years.

Not only was she the last submarine in the Command to mount a deck gun at sea, but she was the last of the submarines designed during the Second World War. She was one of 46 proposed A Class submarines ordered during the latter part of the war for Pacific operations, of which only 16 were completed for peacetime service. She was laid down at the Vickers yard at Barrow in August 1945, launched in 1946 and first commissioned in 1948. Her 4-inch gun mounted forward of the conning-tower was fired for the last time on 3 December 1974, and in a signal to FO Submarines the Captain reported: 'The reek of cordite has passed from the Submarine Service. Last gun action conducted at 03 13.30 Zulu. Time to first round 36 seconds. May the art of the submarine gunnery rest in peace but never be forgotten.'

On 15 June 1953, she set a 'snort' record for British submarines when she voyaged 2,500 nautical miles underwater from Bermuda to the English Channel, in 15 days. Later, during an eventful 11 years in the Far East, from 1958–69, she 'starred' in *On the Beach* when commanded by Gregory Peck, and also appeared as a German submarine in the famous BBC TV series *Warship*. In 1973, the *Andrew*

was 'caught' in the nets of a Teignmouth trawler the *Emma Will* in the Channel. The trawler was towed backwards and called for help from the coastguard before the submarine surfaced to provide the biggest 'one that got away' story in the Devon trawler's history.

HMS *Andrew* served with the Plymouth-based 2nd Submarine Squadron after her return from the Far East, and for the last two years, with her crew of five officers and 63 ratings, provided submarine training for the surface fleet. She paid her last visit to London on 10 December 1974 when she arrived and berthed alongside the cruiser HMS *Belfast* in the Pool of London, and sailed for the last time on 16 December.

At the Royal Navy Submarine Memorial Museum, Gosport, Hants, where *Holland No. 1* is on display is another veteran, *Alliance*. In August 1979, the *Alliance* was towed into No. 4 dock at Southampton for a general exterior overhaul and to fill the ballast tanks with concrete. The work was carried out by Vosper Ship-repairers Limited. Later, the *Alliance* was taken to Gosport where she was hauled ashore and supported on concrete cradles. Following extensive interior work, the submarine was opened to the public. HMS *Alliance* was the oldest A Class submarine afloat – the final link between the submarines of the First and Second World Wars. She has open-type switchboards and control panels, mechanical gauges and 'order' instruments. She was laid down on 13 March 1945, and first commissioned on 14 May 1947.

5
POST-WAR DEVELOPMENTS

Evolved from the T Class, the Porpoise Class were the first 'attack' submarines designed after the Second World War to be accepted into service. Designed for continuous patrols throughout the world, they were capable of long endurance on the surface and submerged, with maximum stress laid on hull strength for great diving depths and near silent operation.

Twin turbocharged ASR1 diesel–electrics developing 3,300 bhp drive twin shafts to give a surface speed of 12 knots, and two main motors produced 5,000 hp to give an underwater speed of 17 knots. The schnorkel equipment was designed to give maximum battery-charging operation even in rough seas. Sea and surface warning radar could be operated at periscope depth whilst air purification by carbon dioxide and hydrogen eliminators made it possible to remain submerged for days at a time. Large storage spaces for supplies, and sea-water distillation plants, made it possible for them to remain on patrol for weeks without support ships. Strip lighting and full air-conditioning added to the high standards of accommodation for the 71 officers and men.

The original eight were *Porpoise, Grampus* and *Rorqual,* completed in 1958, with *Cachalot, Finwhale, Narwhal, Sealion* and *Walrus* completed between 1959 and 1961.

Like the O Class which followed with completion dates from 1960 (*Orpheus*) to November 1967 (*Onyx*), they had much-improved detection equipment and were armed with eight 21-inch torpedo tubes – six bow and two stern – with 30 torpedoes carried.

Both classes were equipped to fire homing torpedoes but in the Oberons, for the first time, some plastic was used in the construction of the superstructure. The glass fibre laminates were mainly used fore and aft of the bridge. In the *Orpheus,* the superstructure was mainly of light alloy aluminium.

Automatic depth-keeping, and steering with complex fire-control equipment for the homing torpedoes, made it possible to reduce the crew to 68.

The badge of Fort Blockhouse, former headquarters of Submarine Command.

The deadly bows of HM Submarine *Onyx*.

Left top: HMS *Dolphin*, Gosport, base of SM1 (First Submarine Squadron).
Left centre: A crewman is winched down on HMAS *Onslow*.
Left bottom: HMS *Porpoise* surfacing.
Above: HMS *Otus* surfacing.

137

Ratings at work in the forward torpedo compartment of a modern O Class submarine.

In March 1965, the *Opossum*, a conventional submarine, achieved the farthest north. It is seen surfaced in the Arctic pack-ice. Grouped below are Lt-Cdr W. L. Owen, Commander of the *Opossum*, and members of the crew ashore on the pack-ice.

Wessex helicopters of 820 Squadron hover over HM Submarine *Otter*.

The *Narwhal* (above) during her visit to Amsterdam in 1974, and the *Finwhale* during a visit to Hong Kong in 1971.

Somewhere in the Atlantic, an RAF Nimrod aircraft keeps a rendezvous with two conventional British submarines.

This picture (above) gives some idea of the complex equipment in the nerve centre of even a conventional submarine. It is reproduced by courtesy of Vickers Limited and was taken in the *Ocelot* in 1970. The stern view of the *Onyx* (right) shows the attention paid to streamlining of the hull for optimum performance.

The Only Dangerous Enemy

The most dangerous enemy of the modern deep-diving submarine is another submarine able to stalk it beneath the sea and sink it with torpedoes.

Until the end of the Second World War, the submarine's primary task was the destruction of enemy merchant shipping carrying the vital raw materials and food essential for the war effort. The military situation today, with its power groupings of the Warsaw Pact and NATO, has resulted in new strategies and tactics to meet the changed conditions. In any crisis situation, the Warsaw Pact maritime lines of communication would be almost non-existent and would carry only a small percentage of the supplies sent in by land. The submarine's main task is now seen as the destruction of surface warships and enemy submarines.

The Vickers-designed Type 2400, the follow-on to the older Porpoise and Oberon Classes, is typical of new designs. The older Porpoise and Oberon boats were large-displacement vessels designed for long endurance patrols across the oceans of the world. Their bulk made them easier to detect, they were fitted with stern tubes – now unnecessary in this modern age of sophisticated wire-guided and homing torpedoes – and their large, highly skilled crews were a drain

The hull lines of the *Oberon* (left) were a compromise between the earlier wartime submarines designed for high surface speeds and the hydrodynamic hull of modern submarines designed for high underwater speeds, with the handling characteristics of a modern aircraft. Although the large number of torpedoes carried allowed long 'interdiction cruises', pure homing-torpedoes are difficult to use against high-performance surface ships, because of the distance at which the target must be engaged.

on available manpower. However, Britain has neither the resources nor the money to build nuclear-powered Fleet submarines in sufficient numbers, and anyway, the application of nuclear power to submarines must result in large displacement and high initial and through life costs, with the associated heavy demands on training, support and logistics. So, new designs for conventional submarines combining deep diving and high underwater speeds with greater underwater endurance and sophisticated weaponry were formulated.

Designed jointly by Vickers and MOD(Navy), with an eye on the overseas market where countries with long coastlines to protect will need long endurance submarines to protect their interests, the Type 2400 is the first new design of conventional submarine for the Royal Navy since the post-war Porpoise and Oberon Classes. At the time of going to press, Vickers are expected to get the first order by mid-1983 after which they would tender for follow-on boats to replace the present force of 15 conventional submarines, in competition with other shipyards. The Type 2400 should cost about £90m and will be capable of using all new weapons.

The new submarine will be the fastest conventional submarine in the world with an underwater speed in excess of 20 knots. The crew of 46, compared with the 68 of the Oberons, and the cost should be less than that of a Fleet submarine. They will be armed with six 21-inch bow torpedo tubes and carry 12 reloads housed in shock-proof pallets, with an associated handling system for rapid reloading. Capable of handling all modern underwater weapons including Harpoon, a power handling system allows fast embarkation of weapons, including mines, with a minimum of danger to personnel and of damage to the weapons themselves.

The modern, sophisticated anti-submarine weapons demand that a submarine spend most of its patrol time deep down or 'snorting'. This in turn imposes a design requirement for the highest underwater performance, and the adoption of single-skin hulls with a high beam-to-length ratio not only gives high manoeuvrability but gives space for two or more decks. Both radiated and self-noise have been reduced considerably compared with the older classes, but high shock resistance has still been retained by careful design.

The Type 2400s have a length of 230 ft compared with the 295 ft of the Oberons, and although shorter displace approximately the same submerged, 2,450 ton. The length of the pressure hull is only 156 ft, and is built of high-tensile steel stiffened by frames of the same material. The fore and after ends terminate in domed bulkheads. The forward external hull – housing the torpedo tubes, Nos 1 and 2 main

ballast tanks, passive sonar array, anchor and cable – is built of high-quality steel except for the portion next to the sonar array, which is glass-reinforced plastic (GRP). The torpedo tubes pass through the upper part of No. 1 tank and torpedoes emerge via independently operated bow shutters linked to the torpedo discharge system and shaped to fit the streamlining of the bow.

The after external hull houses Nos 3 and 4 main ballast tanks with the extreme end aft, containing the bearings, shafts and operating gear for the after hydroplanes and rudders, being free-flooding. The single propeller shaft runs the full length of this structure through a steel tube.

The bridge fin is built of GRP on a steel supporting structure and houses the masts, upper bearings of the twin periscopes, snort induction and exhaust masts, communication and radar masts, and also provides a forward navigating position. It also contains the Omega navigation aerial, active sonar and passive sonar transducers. The superstructure which is contoured round the bridge fin, acts as a streamlined cover for the pressure hull hatches, escape towers and exhaust lines, and gives space for the mooring gear, sonar arrays and indicator buoys.

The pressure hull is divided into three watertight compartments by two transverse watertight bulkheads and the two forward compartments are two-deck, with three hatches giving external access.

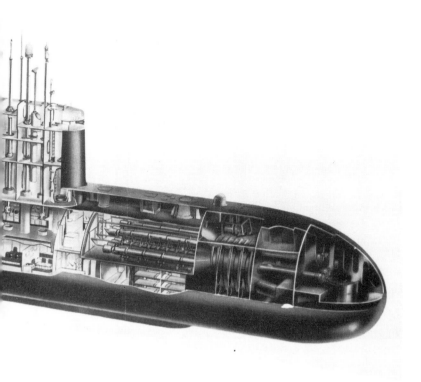

The torpedo embarkation hatch is set at an angle to the forward dome.
The battery-loading hatch at the forward end of the compartment also
provides for general access, and the last opening is part of the one-man
escape tower. The upper level, or No. 1 deck, is the torpedo reload
space and the No. 2 deck (below) provides crew accommodation, sonar
consoles, cold and cool rooms, officers' and ratings' bathrooms,
torpedo operating tanks and torpedo discharge equipment.

The middle compartment No. 1 deck houses the control room,
communications and electronic support measures (ESM) offices and
the CO's cabin. Two hatches provide external access. The one forward
leads to the five-man escape chamber and navigation position on the
bridge. The other, which is the main personnel access hatch at the rear
of the compartment, also provides a battery loading position. The No.
2 deck level comprises the auxiliary machinery and more
accommodation space. Accommodation is to the usual high standards
expected in a modern warship, with showers, WCs and washbasins,
and the modern galley has an electric range, deep-fryer, baking oven
and grill, sink and refrigerator. There are cold, cool and dry stores for
provisions.

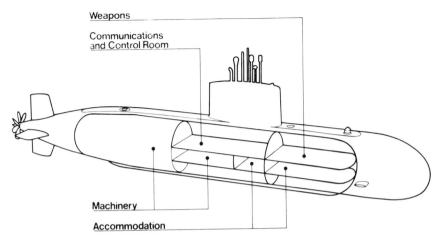

Weapons

Communications
and Control Room

Machinery

Accommodation

A diesel–electric propulsion system is fitted, driving a single fixed-pitch propeller on a shaft driven directly by a twin-armature 4,800-kW electric motor. The two diesel engines developing 1,350 bkW, each drive a sea-water cooled 1.25-MW a.c. generator with built-in rectification, provide the power for charging the batteries when snorting or on the surface. The main batteries consist of two 240-cell sections, each weighing 138 ton. Designed diving depth is in excess of 650 ft.

Two chilled-water plants supply chilled water for air-conditioning and weapon cooling, and a desalination plant supplies 35 gallons an hour of fresh water to supplement that carried in the storage tanks. CO_2 absorption units and oxygen generators form part of the life-support system. A high degree of automation provides among other things, depth and course control, main motor speed, battery charging, and selected systems such as trim. A comprehensive warning and alarm system is also fitted. The Action Information Organisation and Fire Control system is a multi-display system with high computer capacity. Twin computers drive three display consoles and there is a large-scale Tactical Auto-Plot. A digital data system caters for the flow of information between sensors and operators. Omega and Decca Navigation systems and an electromagnetic log are also fitted.

While Type 2400 progressed, the post-war torpedo development programme ran into difficulties, and it was not until late in 1981 that the Government finally announced that they had selected the newly designed Marconi Space and Defence Systems'(MSDS) heavyweight torpedo for the Navy's submarines in preference to the American rival. The primary anti-submarine armament today is the Mk 24 Tigerfish which has replaced the old Mk 23 in the Royal Navy's Fleet and patrol submarines. The Admiralty Underwater Weapons Establishment (AUWE) supported by other Government departments and industry worked out the basic design, but in September 1969, engineering developments were given to MSDS working with AUWE, under the Navy's Director General Weapons (DGW), and a newly formed Torpedo Project Executive. After some 400 test firings the four-year programme ended with MSDS becoming the prime contractor for production and in-service support. Tigerfish became operational in 1974 and is probably the quietest torpedo of its type in the world. It has a fully automatic three-dimensional acoustic homing terminal following a wire-guided run to the target, and does not advertise its presence until the reaction time left to the target submarine makes avoidance tactics impossible.

Propulsion is by a contra-rotating d.c. motor powered by silver-zinc batteries, and with direct drive to contra-rotating propellers. It is designed by the Admiralty Research Laboratory (ARL) for minimum noise and maximum efficiency. The batteries can be connected in series or parallel to give two speeds and the slower speed allows a long endurance and almost noiseless approach to the target area. The 'warshot' version is fitted with primary batteries which have their electrolyte stored in sealed containers for maximum safety and long life.

The outer propeller shaft drives a rotary pump to provide hydraulic power for the rudders and elevators fitted to the cruciform tail surfaces. Roll stabilization is by stub wings fitted in the centre section of the torpedo which are automatically deployed after discharge and these carry ailerons operated by an electrical servo loop. The aluminium alloy hull is streamlined to minimize noise and drag, and is treated against salt-water corrosion. This enables the weapon to be kept in a flooded tube at instant readiness.

When discharged by compressed air or water ram jet, or when it is 'swum out', the torpedo is normally guided by the fire-control computer operator to the target area. He can also send commands to and receive information back from the torpedo by means of the wire-guided link, which allows targets at long range to be attacked. A single-core insulated wire is used and is dispensed from the torpedo – via a hollow tube in the propeller shaft – and from the submarine itself, so that it is not strained by being pulled through the water. The cruise speed is in excess of 30 knots.

The GEC-Marconi Electronics Company, of which MSDS is a part, has been involved in the design of the acoustic homing torpedo since

1943, including the Mk 20 of the early 1950s and the similar Mk 23 which had wire-guided facilities. This led in turn to the early work on Tigerfish in 1957 and the need for the first time of both an active and passive homing head, with a proportional control system.

Potential submarine targets over the next 20 years must become faster, deeper diving, quieter, more manoeuvrable and therefore much harder to destroy. Diving depths in excess of 2600 ft are certain. At the same time, the torpedo's kill potential, speed and depth of operation, are the least flexible of the general performance parameters. The advent of the micro-chip gave the designer the first chance to break out of the circle imposed by so many conflicting factors. A large computing capability gives the torpedo the chance to react in real-time, to every variable. This led to an increased search 'volume' and

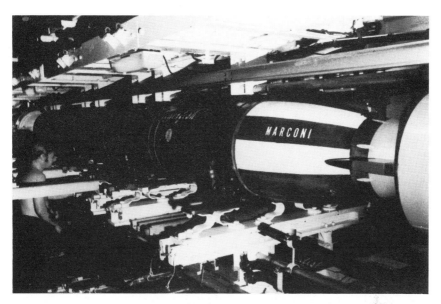

Shown here are different views of the Tigerfish torpedo during manufacture at the GEC-Marconi factory.

greater reliability. Modern electrically powered torpedoes using the new Lucas-designed contra-rotating motor which has a very high power output, brought the density/volume ratio closer to that of the thermal engine, typically some 4 kW/kg.

Naval Staff Requirement 7525 called for a torpedo to replace the Tigerfish, the MOD version of which entered service in 1974 and the improved Mod. 1 type being accepted by the Navy in 1980. The new weapon will arm the Polaris (Trident) submarines, and the Fleet and patrol submarines like the Type 2400, the main function of which will be to destroy enemy submarines. A secondary function will be to attack surface ships at less than the range of the new sub-Harpoon missile.

It is suggested that the new heavyweight torpedo should be able to sink a ship of up to 40,000 ton with its powerful blast warhead. It is approximately 26 ft long, 21 in in diameter and weighs some 795 lb in water. It can be fired at any point over a wide range of operating depths, and at slower speeds of about 20 knots it is believed to have a range in excess of 20 miles. It has five times the computing capacity of the highly successful lightweight Sting Ray torpedo, and a 5 million bit storage capacity. Information is passed both ways as normal through wire guidance, and the torpedo's own array allows it to continue the attack

153

Tigerfish being loaded in HMS *Conqueror*, which sank the Argentine cruiser *Belgrano* – with an early mark of torpedo – and (right) the *Swiftsure* at high speed.

even if the guidance wire should snap. In the search area, the torpedo assumes a glide angle from its 164 ft approach depth and at slow speed classifies the target by noise characteristics and behaviour. Originally designed for speeds in excess of 50 knots it was updated to counter the new Alpha Class Soviet submarine.

It has been reported that the new giant Soviet submarines have double hulls with an estimated 12–13 ft between the hulls, and it is well known that the effective hitting power of a torpedo is inversely proportional to this 'stand-off' distance. The new weapon has therefore been designed with a direct energy charge.

Although technical experts in industry and the Navy knew a great deal about the application of nuclear power to maritime propulsion, the Admiralty's main research effort after the war focused on the use of concentrated hydrogen peroxide as a power source for high submerged speeds.

Even before the First World War, the Germans had experimented with closed-cycle propulsion systems which needed no air, and would permit the building of a true submarine able to remain underwater for long periods. During the Second World War, they began trials with a system designed by Professor Hellmuth Walther using hydrogen peroxide, pumped from tanks and passed through a catalyst. It broke down into its constituent parts in a reaction chamber and the hot gases were expanded through a steam turbine driving a single propeller. Very high power was available from a small, compact propulsion plant which needed no air and left no visible trail in the sea.

The trials submarine reached submerged speeds of up to 28 knots in late 1940 and had submarines like it ever become operational, they would have been a major obstacle to any allied victory. The one snag was that they burnt up fuel very quickly, and only had a radius of action of some 50 miles. A Type XVII submarine was built with a double pressure hull shaped like a figure eight, with the lower part of the eight – and the smaller part – used as a fuel tank. These tall, narrow

Contrasting views of the *Excalibur* showing the streamlined hull and stern.

boats were not much good in a seaway but the performance was outstanding. With 40 ton of fuel, they could reach 26 knots over a distance of 80 miles.

The modified Type XVIIB (*U1405–1407*) had a range of 120 miles at 21.5 knots and it was *U1407*, scuttled off Cuxhaven when the war ended, that was raised and salvaged by the British. The *U1407* was salvaged in 1946 and renamed HMS *Meteorite*.

The famous engineer of the *Tally-Ho*, Peter Scott Maxwell, was sent to Germany to supervise the departure of the submarine for Britain and remained there for several months to acquire a complete set of spares and the prototype of a larger engine. Mr E. Davies, the then head of Vicker's Internal Combustion Engine drawing office also visited Germany, to advise on development work by Vickers for the Hydrogen Test Peroxide (HTP) method of propulsion.

Subsequently, Vickers built the two submarines HMS *Excalibur* and *Explorer*. These were 225.5 ft long, with a beam of 15.75 ft and a draught of 11 ft. The *Explorer* was launched on 5 March 1954 and completed 28 November 1956. The *Excalibur* was launched on 25 February 1955 and completed 22 March 1958. The *Explorer* was the first new submarine to be built for the Royal Navy since the A Class of 1947.

Although able to sustain high submerged speeds of over 25 knots for short distances, they were still not true submarines and were very noisy, and HTP was a highly volatile fuel. The *Explorer* was dubbed 'Exploder' by her crew because of the fireballs ejected from the exhaust when she was started up.

Although both joined the Fleet, with the *Explorer* serving until 1962 and *Excalibur* until 1965, their only purpose was to provide operational experience for their Walthur turbine plant, and to act as high-speed underwater targets for anti-submarine warfare training.

The *Excalibur* cost £1,142,000. Her main turbines were powered by steam and carbon dioxide produced by burning diesel oil in an atmosphere of steam and oxygen formed from the decomposition of high-test hydrogen peroxide. Full power was available when submerged without the need for air. Secondary propulsion was also available – diesel or electric batteries – for slower speeds.

The conclusions were inescapable and the Admiralty decided to go nuclear. There were two options – buy American or build British but wait for a reactor of new design. Lord Mountbatten at the Admiralty found the buy American argument the more persuasive and authority was given for talks to begin with the American Government.

A Remarkable Reaction

In 1931, Cockroft and Walton produced the world's first artificial nuclear reaction when they smashed a lithium nucleus using a new research tool, the particle accelerator. The following year James Chadwick discovered the nuclear trigger, the neutron.

Hahn and Strassman's experiments almost went unnoticed due to the war in Europe – but not by Einstein, who wrote to President Theodore Roosevelt warning of the terrible dangers from a chain reaction weapon. The outcome was Fermi's historic nuclear 'pile' in Chicago and the Manhattan Project, which produced the first atomic weapon and the first generation of nuclear reactors.

In 1948, the reactor revolution began with the new revolutionary submarine ordered by the then Vice-Admiral H. G. Rickover. It was to be driven by a compact nuclear plant that would need no refuelling for years, drive the submarine at high underwater speeds, and enable it to seek out and destroy an enemy target before defensive action could be taken.

Neutrons are heavy, uncharged atomic particles. Each uranium nucleus emits 2.5 neutrons as it degenerates after splitting, and this results in a continuous, self-supporting chain reaction in a critical mass of fissionable uranium 235. In theory, one pound weight of this uranium can produce the equivalent energy that could be obtained from 1,000 ton of high-quality coal. This is due to the loss of weight by the nuclear fragments, and Einstein's theory states that the energy is proportional to the mass loss, multiplied by the square of the velocity of light.

Since 1947, the USN had pioneered an intensive engineering survey into the ideal hull design for submarines under the acronym of GUPPY (Greater Underwater Propulsion Programme). The optimum shape was found to be a tear-drop form, with bluff bows, a circular mid-section and a long tapered stern. The traditional conning-tower was replaced by the sail or fin, like the dorsal fin of a fish. A new type of submarine was built at the Portsmouth Yard, New Hampshire, and was commissioned on 5 December 1953. The USS *Albacore* was powered by massed banks of silver-zinc batteries driving contra-rotating twin propellers, and during trials she reached 33 knots submerged.

During extensive trials it was also found that the designers had achieved the optimum position for the control surfaces. The submarine could turn and bank underwater like an aeroplane in the sky. All subsequent submarines have been designed around the Albacore hull.

In 1950, Rickover was head of the newly formed Naval Reactors Branch of the US Atomic Energy Commission and the decision was taken to build two prototype submarines, one with a Pressure Water Reactor (PWR) in which the hot core of enriched uranium is cooled by a closed circuit using water under very high pressure. The other was cooled by liquid sodium metal to extract the heat, at a higher rate and temperature.

The PWR reactor was used to power the world's first nuclear-propelled submarine, the USS *Nautilus*, built by the Electric Boat Company and commissioned on 30 September 1954. On 17 January 1955, *Nautilus* originated the famous signal: 'Underway on nuclear power'. Her first core took her 62,560 miles, her second 93,000 miles and her third 158,000 miles. The historic 1958 voyage from Hawaii to Portland, England, took her under the ice and directly under the North Pole.

In 1956, the Government had asked Vickers, Rolls-Royce and Foster Wheeler, to combine in building a prototype nuclear reactor. A new company, Vickers Nuclear Engineering, was formed to control policy. A welcome injection of nuclear 'know-how' from America followed the talks between President Dwight Eisenhower and Prime Minister Harold Macmillan in Bermuda, from 21–24 March 1958. Agreement was reached with the American Government for the UK to purchase a complete set of nuclear propulsion machinery as used in the USS *Skipjack*.

The US Skipjack Class of attack submarines were the fastest then in combat service with the USN, using an advanced second-generation reactor – the Westinghouse S5W – driving a single propeller at the tip of the stern. Although maximum operational speeds are classified, it is assumed that they are faster than the original *Albacore*'s speed of 33 knots and have a top speed of some 40 knots.

The Westinghouse Electric Corporation and the Electric Boat Company, as American designers of the hull and reactor, signed an agreement with Rolls-Royce Associates and Foster Wheeler, who designed the pressure vessel and associated equipment. The decision to buy American, which was approved by Admiral of The Fleet Earl Mountbatten, enabled Britain to get her first nuclear-powered submarine, HMS *Dreadnought*, to sea three years earlier than anticipated, and led to completion of the British prototype propulsion plant at Dounreay.

The amount of uranium used in the fuel elements inside the heavily

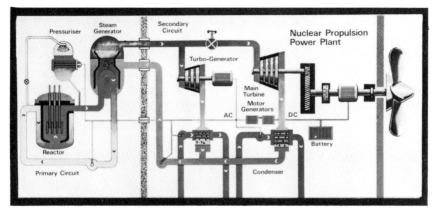

Nuclear Propulsion Power Plant

shielded pressure chamber of a pressurized water reactor is so small that it could be compressed into a small pot. Yet the enormous amount of energy generated gives the submarine almost unlimited endurance and provides not only the propulsion power, but all the electrical power required by the vessel. The fission process providing the energy is controlled by neutron-absorbing rods which are inserted into the fuel elements.

The reactor, steam generator, pressurizer and coolant pumps and pipes, form an enclosed loop known as the primary circuit. Water pumped through this loop passes through the reactor which is so hot that the water could boil, and the steam produced could cause unstable conditions. Electrical heaters inserted through the walls of the pressurizer form a steam bubble which maintains the system at the right saturation level.

After passing through the reactor, the hot coolant water circulates through the steam generator, where the heat is used to convert the low-pressure water outside the tubes into high-quality steam. The cooled primary water is recirculated through the reactor to continue the heat-exchange cycle. The whole primary circuit is built inside a heavily shielded reactor compartment to protect the crew from radiation.

The secondary circuit now comes into operation. Steam is used to drive the ahead and astern main turbines, through clutch, gears and the single propeller shaft. The spent steam is condensed in a sea-water cooler and returned to the steam generator as water, to begin the secondary cycle again.

The steam also drives turbo-generators to provide electrical a.c. supplies, and spent steam from these is also condensed and returned to the steam generators. Motor generators or batteries provide the d.c. power requirements.

161

The *Valiant* leaving Singapore.

Highly accurate automatic and manual controls, together with sophisticated electronic and mechanical 'fail-safe' features, control the reactor and steam-generating processes, and assure reactor safety at all times.

On 16 November 1960, the first RN Nuclear Monitoring Team of an officer and four ratings completed training and became operational as a mobile unit. Most of their training was at the RN Electrical School HMS *Collingwood*, Fareham, Hants. The first team was posted to the American Polaris base at Holy Loch.

Basically, today as then, the teams are concerned with commonsense precautions for the operation of nuclear-powered ships using UK ports. Nuclear radiation is unseen and can't be smelt, and sensitive instruments are needed to point out dangerous levels of radiation. They can accurately assess and control radiation hazards in the unlikely event of an accident, and are available for consultation with local authorities. Safety figures to which the teams work, are more stringent than those laid down by the International Committee on Radiological Protection, and the Medical Research Council.

Among the many engineering problems this new power source brought to the Navy were the specifications needed to ensure the safety of the reactor plant, the men working on the plant, and those serving at sea. To maintain the specifications throughout, a refit requires constant monitoring of the work, materials and processes used. This is the job of the Nuclear Standards Branch.

The first docking of the *Valiant*, 1967–8, provided their first training ground. In 1968, when Mr Myles Crowder was appointed Assistant Nuclear Power Manager, new staff were recruited and trained, special tools and equipment purchased, and a technically expert and competent team built up.

There is constant monitoring of production centres concerned and during a major refit, entry to the reactor compartment is authorized by a Duty Inspector. The all-welded stainless-steel reactor primary plant must not be left unsealed for long, as foreign bodies could enter causing failure when the plant becomes operational. Airtight polythene tents are often used to maintain cleanliness but the work does involve cuts being made in this protective covering and requires the use of mirrors for inspection and checks.

The sealed condition of the system must be maintained, however, even after cuts are made, and cloth covered sponges are carefully inserted into the cuts after the work for which they were made has been finished. They are even more carefully checked afterwards to ensure that one has not been lost.

163

The Royal Naval Armament Depot at Coulport was built and is responsible for the Polaris A3 missiles, including receipt, storage, maintenance, supply and issue, under a superintendent who works indirectly to Director General Weapons, Navy. He accepts the missiles into service, and has responsibility for ensuring that the missiles and torpedoes produced in UK depots are fit for service.

On 30 June 1966, the RN Polaris School was opened at Faslane. The 1966–7 Estimates included £58 m for its construction and for that at Coulport. This magnificent school built on the side of Gareloch was the responsibility of the famous Wimpey firm. The six-storey structure was constructed of vibration-free reinforced concrete and is complete with a penthouse lecture theatre.

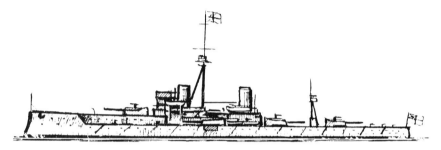

The Dreadnought Saga

The name 'Dreadnought', chosen for the Navy's first nuclear-powered submarine, evoked nostalgic memories of Jackie Fisher's Dreadnoughts. Armed with ten 13.5-inch or 12-inch guns, and carrying a secondary armament of twelve 6-inch or up to eighteen 4-inch guns, they had made every capital ship in the world obsolete.

The Dreadnoughts of that era – and there were 20 in the First Fleet at the beginning of the First World War – were as outstanding an advance in the history of battleship-building as was HMS *Dreadnought* in the history of the design and construction of submarines.

When the then Admiralty placed the order for the submarine with the Vickers Shipbuilding Group, it not only put the Royal Navy firmly on a nuclear course, but took the company into the world of nuclear engineering. A move which has proved of immeasurable value to them. As a bonus, it also renewed an old, established working relationship with the English Boat Company of America, with whom they had worked during the building of the Navy's first Holland Class submarine in 1901. It also took the elite of the Navy's sailors, the submariners, into the world of nuclear physics which would result in a new generation of steam-raising machinery for their first true submarines – ones able to roam the oceans of the world at great depths, high speeds and with almost unlimited endurance. In fact the only limits would be human frailty and the amount of food that could be carried.

Ordered in 1959 and laid down that year on 12 June, HRH Prince Philip placed the first section on the berth by moving a handle, which operated a gamma-ray beam to turn a winch and draw a 30-ft cylindrical section of the hull into position.

Although it was the submarines that captured the headlines, there was a continuous building programme from 1957, to provide the shore-based support facilities needed for experiments and training.

The Dounreay prototype reactor when first installed. Experiments here later produced an advanced long-life reactor core for the Navy.

Great Britain had developed a reactor technology of her own at Harwell, and a Naval Reactor Team was formed in 1954 to turn theory into practice. The result was the Neptune reactor used to investigate core physics, geometrical shapes and fuel burn-up. In 1957, it was decided to build a prototype reactor and propulsion plant at Dounreay. It commissioned the same year under a Captain RN as Superintendent and was operated by Rolls-Royce Associates.

Opened by the Queen Mother in May 1968, the £47m Clyde Submarine Base HMS *Neptune* at Faslane, on the Gareloch incorporates the RN Armament Depot at Coulport, Loch Long.

Faslane consists of the dockyard, with jetties and a floating dock providing alongside support for submarines; associated command and administration buildings; workshops, effluent disposal plant and standby generation stations. The barracks area includes married quarters at Helensburgh and Rhu for some 1,200 officers and men. There is a recreational area with floodlit soccer pitches and an indoor sports facility with a heated swimming-pool, a 4,000-seat cinema, shopping arcade, NAAFI supermarket, tailor, bank, library – just about every modern amenity for the 7,000 Navy personnel and MOD (Navy) civilians, who work alongside each other.

In overall charge is Commodore Clyde who is also Commodore of the base and Commanding Officer of HMS *Neptune*. The 10th Submarine Squadron comprises the four Polaris submarines; the 3rd Submarine Squadron, the nuclear-powered Fleet and the conventionally powered patrol submarines. Each squadron is commanded by a Captain (S/M), and Captain 10th Submarine

Squadron (S/M 10) is also the Queen's Harbourmaster and responsible for the waters contained inside some 60 miles of coastline, the Clyde and associated lochs. Other support facilities include a stores complex handling over 100,000 different items, a fuel depot, transport department, a diving team and a comprehensive health safety organization.

During the 20-month building period, 100,000 cubic yards of solid rock were blasted away and 30,000 square yards of shuttering were used. Some 850 miles of wiring and 30,000 separate connections made up the complex. Present at the opening ceremony was Admiral Levering Smith USN, Director of the Special Project Office, and the unstinting help given by the USN included the training of instructors, and the weapon crews of the *Renown* and *Resolution*, at the Guided Missile School, Dam Neck, Virginia.

On the other side of Scotland at the Rosyth Naval Base, the dockyard was extensively equipped to provide a nuclear refitting capability. It was to be the refitting yard for all Polaris submarines, but it was decided to precede this, to gain experience, by the first refit of the first nuclear-powered British submarine, HMS *Dreadnought*.

Lastly, the Nuclear Submarine Refitting Facility was built at Chatham Dockyard, which had a history of building 57 submarines going back to the *C17* in 1908. Conspicuous by the tall accommodation block and 120-ton cranes, which are essential for the refit and refuelling of the new capital ships, the facility was custom-built using Nos 6 and 7 dry docks and adjacent dock sides. There are workshops, power houses, offices and living quarters for the submarine crews. Submarines arrive without weapons to have their old reactor cores removed and replaced with new ones.

In 1969, defence cuts in the White Paper led to a slowing down of the nuclear building programme, and the government decided that Vickers would take over all future building of nuclear-propelled submarines, as the sole contractor. John Morris, Minister of Defence (Equipment) said in the House on 4 March 1969: 'Our future building programme can support only one yard and Vickers were chosen because of their clear lead in design capability and experience.'

Prime Minister Harold Wilson was reported in *Hansard* on 27 March 1969, as saying: 'The decision was based on sound economic reasons and taken in the knowledge of Vickers' greater experience and capacity in all aspects of the work.' Thus Vickers became, and still is, the only builder of nuclear submarines in the UK and will obviously be the main contractor for the Trident programme.

Polaris and Fleet submarine costs reported in *Hansard* 26 February

The momentous occasion of a royal launch at Barrow.

1969 were: *Resolution* £40.2 m; *Repulse* £37.5 m, *Renown* £39.5 m and *Revenge* £38.6 m; *Dreadnought* £18.5 m, *Valiant* £24.9 m and *Warspite* £21.5 m.

A tribute must be paid to the American Government and their major contractors who so readily placed their knowledge at the disposal of the Admiralty. The Westinghouse Electric Corporation and the Electric Boat Division of the General Dynamics Corporation provided training facilities for Naval personnel and Vickers engineers.

HMS *Dreadnought* was Barrow's 281st submarine for the Royal Navy and her construction posed many new problems which had to be solved. None were greater than the mastering of the new welding techniques required, or the guaranteeing of the watertight integrity of the reactor compartment. The hull was built in 150-ton sections ranging in shape from a cylinder to a cone, and a new floating dock was built to house her while fitting out. The dock and the module repair facility cost £5 m. The latter was towed to Barrow from Portsmouth where it was built. The royal launch by HM The Queen on 21 October 1960, was a momentous occasion. The submarine was 265.5 ft long, 32.25 ft in the beam and had a draught of 26 ft. She displaced 3,556 ton surfaced and 4,064 ton dived. Carrying a crew of 11 officers and 77 men, she was armed with six 21-inch torpedo tubes in the bows. Her first Commanding Officer, Commander B. F. P. Samborne, and her senior ratings, went to America for nuclear training.

The reactor core was loaded in 1962 and went critical later that year. She dived for the first time in Ramsden Dock on 10 January 1963 and commissioned on 17 April 1963, after successful sea trials. The towns of Morecambe and Heysham adopted her and on 29 March 1963, a commemorative scroll was presented to the ship.

High-speed trials revealed that the rudder acted as a diving hydroplane at high speeds. The after end of the submarine housing all the machinery and the manoeuvring room, became known as the American Sector! Electricity could be produced for 1 p a kilowatt but water came more expensive, at $7\frac{1}{2}$ p a gallon.

The *Dreadnought* was to make the news headlines on several occasions. On 21 June 1963 she was ordered to sea from Gibraltar and on 24 June, fired four torpedoes at the drifting and dangerous wreck of the giant *Essenberger Chemist*. Three torpedoes hit and left her just awash, and the sinking was completed by the guns of HMS *Salisbury*.

On 19 September 1967, she left Rosyth for Singapore on a sustained high-speed run. The round trip notched up a record 26,545 miles submerged and 4,640 miles surfaced. On 30 April 1968, the last day of her first commission, she took families to sea off May Island and dived

HMS *Dreadnought* on trials from the base at Faslane and right, in the Straits of Johore, Singapore, during her high-speed record voyage.

with them on board – a unique way to end a commission. After a refit at Rosyth, she recommissioned on 10 September 1970.

During this two-year major refit, the submarine was refuelled with the new British long-life core, and her ballast tank valves were changed to reduce noise. She had also suffered from hairline cracks in some deep welds, which were successfully corrected.

Termed a 'Fleet submarine' because of her ability to operate with surface ships at high speed, she and other Fleet submarines were quickly dubbed 'hunter-killers' by the popular press, as they were equipped for hunting and destroying enemy submarines. To this end, the *Dreadnought* carries powerful sonar arrays high in the modified bluff bows, beneath which are the six torpedo tubes and a magazine with a large reload capacity, for homing or wire-guided torpedoes.

She follows standard American practice, with particular attention being paid to the decoration and furnishing of living and recreational quarters. Unlimited fresh water is provided from distilling plants; varied hot or cold meals come from a modern galley serving meals on a

A lighter moment for *Dreadnought*'s crew. 'Hands to bathe.'

cafeteria system and there are separate messes for senior and junior rates, a library, cinema equipment, and tape recordings. Her three deck levels have ample headroom.

HMS *Dreadnought*, captained by Commander A. G. Kennedy, surfaced through the ice at the North Pole on 3 March 1971. She was under the ice for several days and covered some 1,500 miles in the area, surfacing about six times. The special equipment for measuring her depth under the ice worked perfectly. As the submarine broke through the ice to the surface, it was described as: 'just a shudder like a lift coming to a stop'. The hilly landscape was extremely cold with temperatures of minus 35°F. Polar bears were conspicuous by their absence!

In the Malacca Straits in 1973, when the helicopter cruiser HMS

Commander A. G. Kennedy.

Tiger was leading an Anglo-Dutch squadron, the *Dreadnought* took part in the first major rescue at sea by a nuclear-powered submarine.

The 20,953-ton tanker *Anson* had ripped into the side of the 7,479-ton freighter *Carnation*, and the two had become locked together. The seamen from the crippled freighter took to the boats and 35 were rescued by the submarine. Salvage teams led by Lieutenant P. Tibbenham and Surgeon Lieutenant-Commander R. Harland, were airlifted to the ships by Sea King helicopters of 826 Naval Air Squadron. They rendered first-aid and prevented an explosion of the escaping oil. The survivors were later airlifted from the submarine to the frigate HMS *Rhyl*.

The Admiralty had announced on 31 August 1960 that the contract for a second Fleet submarine had been placed with the Vickers Shipbuilding Group. It was to be slightly larger than the *Dreadnought*, with Rolls-Royce building the 'steam-raising' plant and the English Electric Company building the steam turbines. Named HMS *Valiant*, it was to become the prototype from which all future British-built Fleet submarines were developed. Vickers were fast expanding their nuclear knowledge and their experts, led by Mr Leonard Redshaw – the company's Chief Polaris Executive – made frequent visits to the States to discuss problems with their American colleagues of the Electric Boat Company. Within a few years, with the Fleet submarines HMS *Warspite* and *Churchill* already ordered from them, they were confronted with new problems following the signing of the Polaris Sales Agreement between the American and British Governments. Two of these giants – virtually Fleet submarines, but with a missile section inserted – were ordered from them as lead yard. It was an

HMS *Dreadnought* at the scene of the collision, with one tanker embedded in the other.

Survivors from the tanker are taken on board HMS *Dreadnought*.

immense challenge to the Barrow yard's manpower and organization.

The *Valiant* was 285 ft long with a beam of 33.25 ft. She was launched at Barrow on 3 December 1963 by Mrs Thorneycroft, wife of Mr Peter Thorneycroft MP, then Minister for Defence. Like her predecessor, *Valiant* was fitted with an inertial navigation system, equipment for measuring her depth under ice, long range sonars and first class accommodation. She had a crew of 11 officers and 79 ratings. Her first Captain was Commander P. G. M. Herbert, formerly Commander of the patrol submarine HMS *Porpoise*.

On 25 April 1967, the *Valiant* returned from exercises in the Far East. She made the 12,000 mile return journey from Singapore submerged, a record underwater voyage for a British submarine at that time. On the outward journey in the February, she had surfaced only once at Mauritius to give the crew a rest and recreation break.

The *Valiant* and *Warspite*, the first fitted with the British-designed long-life nuclear core, were the first class of Fleet submarine designed with experience gained in the *Dreadnought*. They were followed by the

Loading a torpedo through the forward hatch of a Fleet submarine. The Swiftsure Class were the first to be armed with the new Mk 24 torpedo and can also fire the Harpoon anti-surface missile which has a range in excess of 60 miles.

A view of the torpedo space in the *Dreadnought* and below, a practice torpedo leaving the tube of a submerged submarine. This picture was taken during trials using the Navy's 'free style' diving equipment in the Mediterranean and may well be the first such picture taken

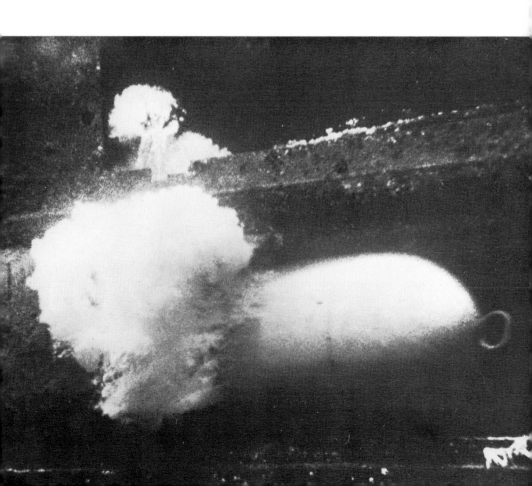

Churchill, Conqueror and *Courageous*. Following these, in 1978, the Swiftsure Class was fitted with an improved Valiant-type propulsion plant. These submarines, like the Churchills, displace 3,500 ton on the surface and 4,500 ton submerged. They are armed with five 21-inch torpedo tubes and are slightly smaller than the Churchills, with a length of 272 ft, a beam of 33.33 ft and a draught of 28 ft.

The enormous fin of HMS *Valiant*.

Part of the Senior Ratings' Mess (above), and one view of the modern, stainless-steel galley.

Switched on for aquabatics! Seen in close-up, the driving seat is very similar to
that in a modern jet aircraft, even down to the joy-stick type of control held in
the hands. These submarines and their successors can turn and bank
underwater just like an aircraft, and crew members at operational positions
are strapped in for safety. They have a smaller turning circle underwater than
a frigate does on the surface. Secret data at the top left-hand side of the picture
were blanked out by special covers for security purposes. There are two seat
positions side by side in these sophisticated underwater capital ships.

The *Valiant* is seen here during high-speed trials with below, a view as seen by the Commanding Officer on the bridge.

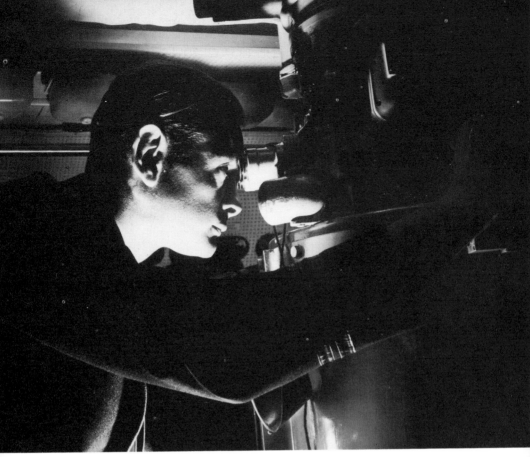

In subdued lighting to preserve night vision, an officer takes a sight through the periscope and below, all that an enemy might glimpse before a surface attack is delivered.

The *Valiant* at high speed.

Swiftsure Class above showing (front to rear) search periscope, radar, radio, ESM. Below (left to right) Soviet Victor periscope, VHF aerial, radar, DF loop and HF aerial. Top right (left to right) Soviet Alpha search and attack periscopes, radar, HF aerial and DF loop, and bottom right *Dreadnought's* search periscope and radio mast.

The 'Eyes' Have It

The length of periscope masts reflects the need for submarines to observe at periscope depth and yet remain safe from damage by ramming. In the Oberons for instance, the mast length is about 40 ft and in the much larger Polaris-missile submarines which tower nearly 60 ft high in dry dock, it seems reasonable to assume they will have masts of about the same height, 60 ft.

Barr and Stround, the famous manufacturers of periscopes, have added the sophistication of laser ranging, light-intensifiers for night observation, thermal-imaging systems with allied video recorders, ESM, radar and radio. Many submarines have masts painted in random colours to reduce the risk of visual detection and many also have schnorkel exhaust and induction masts, the latter drawing air in and the former breathing exhaust gases out. While nuclear submarines make use of electrolysis of distilled sea-water – one pint splits into oxygen and hydrogen sufficient to provide 100 men with enough oxygen for an hour, with the hydrogen being pumped back into the sea – they also have snort masts.

A 'superb' photograph of HM Submarine *Superb* at high speed (left), and a stern-on view of the Spartan (above).

Commander G. R. King, CO of HM Submarine *Valiant* (top left), and
Commander R. N. Buckley, CO of the *Churchill* (below).

The *Conqueror* which sank the Argentine cruiser *Belgrano* during the Falkland
conflict (above).

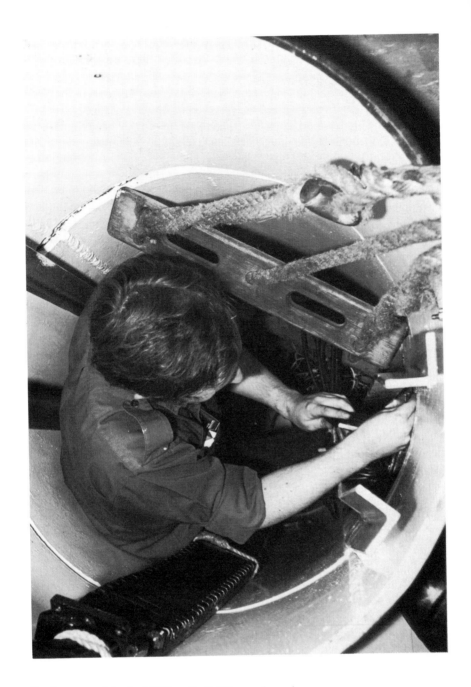

Rating at work in the ESM well of a Fleet submarine.

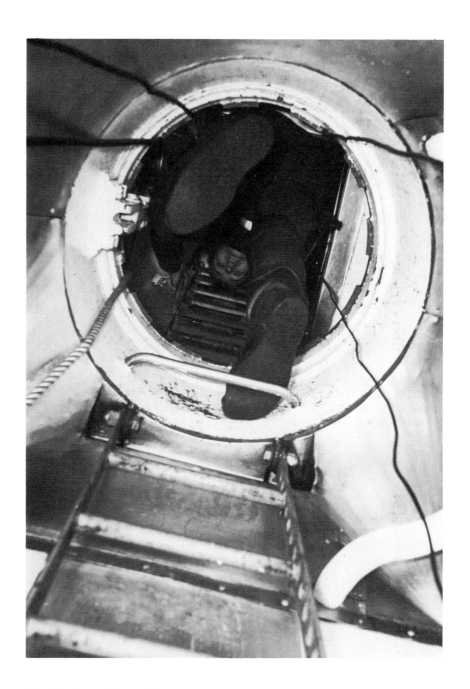

Coming down the conning-tower.

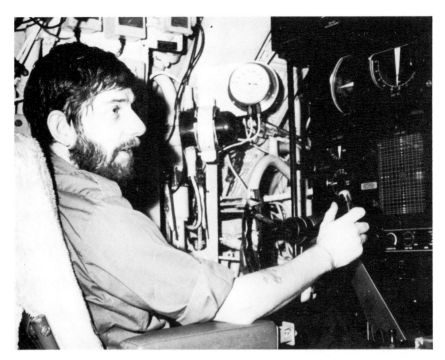

Rating on the after planes (above), and checking the torpedo tubes (below). Loading a Tigerfish torpedo in HMS *Conqueror* (right).

The *Churchill* which recently completed successful test firings of the American-built anti-ship missile Harpoon (right). Like the rest of her class, she may also carry other modern anti-ship/submarine weapon systems.

6

THE ETERNAL VIGIL

In a foreword to the booklet produced by the then Technical Publications Department of the Vickers Shipbuilding Group, Barrow, for HMS *Resolution*, is an apt quotation from the writings of John Philpot Curran, 1750–1817: 'The condition upon which God hath given liberty to man is eternal vigilance; which condition if he break, servitude is at once the consequence of his crime, and the punishment of his guilt.' It was appropriate that the motto chosen for the first British Polaris submarine was 'Resolute and Vigilant'.

In the same booklet, Vice-Admiral Sir Hugh Mackenzie, KCB DSO DSC, then Chief Polaris Executive, wrote expressing his belief in the deterrent: 'The marriage of nuclear power and the ballistic missile has brought about as great a revolution in naval warfare, as in their time, did the introduction of steam, the armour-piercing shell, or the application of electric propulsion to the infant submarine. HMS *Resolution* is the first warship of a new era for the Royal Navy and her role will be quite unlike anything the Navy has ever tackled before.

'Into the *Resolution*, her sister submarines, and their weapon systems has gone a care in design and workmanship of the very highest order, in which the shipbuilders and other contractors have played a most important part. The result is a precision weapon of terrifying power. Upon the known reliability and efficiency of this weapon in service depends its success.

'God grant the weapon may never be used. If it ever has to be used we shall have failed in our duty of preventing war, but the very essence of the deterrent is that it will be ready to work whenever necessary without any risk of failure. No aggressor will be deterred by a threat of retaliation that he believes to be hollow. To believe that he would, is like expecting a First Division team to be worried by a ship's side wearing the cup finalists' jerseys. It is no use just pretending to be able to do the job. The stakes are too high to rely on bluff.

'To fulfil their role, crews of Polaris submarines face a tough challenge, a real task. The instant readiness required will demand of the officers and ratings who man the *Resolution*, exacting standards of performance, of vigilance, and of personal individual responsibility. In achieving these standards, as indeed they will, they can rightly take pride in the service they are carrying out.'

Concentration by many writers on the destructive capability of the

16 A3 missiles – with an explosive power greater than the aggregate of all bombs dropped by both sides during the Second World War – has tended to obscure what was one of the greatest achievements in the history of British shipbuilding.

Following the signing of the Nassau Agreement between President John F. Kennedy and Prime Minister Harold Macmillan on 21 December 1962, it was stated that the RN would have four SSBN (Ship Submersible Ballistic Nuclear) submarines. British-designed and the biggest ever built in the UK, they would use the American weapon system and equipment. The warheads would be built in Britain.

Design work began in January 1963 with Vickers, as the lead yard, building *Resolution* and *Repulse*, and Cammell Laird, *Renown* and *Revenge*. The Government directed that they be deployed by 1968 and built within the budget allocated. On 6 April 1963, the Polaris Sales Agreement was signed, under which the Americans agreed to supply up to 100 missiles less warheads.

Rear-Admiral C. W. H. Shepherd, CB CBE, Deputy Controller (Polaris), wrote in his introduction to *Polaris and The Royal Navy 1963–1973*: 'When the Government gave the Navy the go ahead in January 1963, it specified that the first Polaris submarine should be at sea by 1968. To achieve this goal within the specified time scale needed dedication probably unsurpassed in naval history, considering the number of people and authorities involved on both sides of the Atlantic.

'We planned in 1963 to fire our first missile at 11.15 EST (Eastern Standard Time) on 15 February 1968. We failed to achieve this target by 15 milliseconds. We were told in 1963 that there must be a continuous deterrent from July 1968. We achieved this.'

Vickers were to supply Cammell Laird with specialized materials and training assistance. Before construction began, 500,000 man-hours were spent on planning; 10,000 detailed drawings and 1,000 fully illustrated manuals were produced and checked to ensure the highest standards of accuracy. Over 500 manufacturers were involved and as a preliminary to actual construction, a full-scale mock-up was built to plan the positioning of equipment, routeing of trunking, cables and pipes. The mock-up also allowed the crews to become familiar with every detail of their working environment, so that at the fitting-out berth, as access openings disappeared with startling rapidity, they were able to find their way around with ease and begin their training programmes in earnest.

The Barrow workshops provided in one covered area everything

197

needed to prefabricate the 15 huge sections of the pressure hull, ranging in shape from a cylinder to a cone. Massive rolling shafts rotated the sections to provide the specialist work force with easy access to any particular spot. To the casual onlooker, the scene might have seemed like a shot from a space odyssey film set. Closer inspection would reveal thick hulls of a special steel designed to withstand the enormous pressures at depths of up to 2,000 ft. Some main items were installed before the individual sections were moved the short distance to the berth on a powerful transporter, one of the biggest in the world. At the berth, the sections were welded together using rigidly controlled techniques, specially developed for this thickness of steel.

The fore and aft sections were built up separately but simultaneously, with a space between them into which the missile section, complete with tubes, was fitted. The fin, housing the periscope, masts and bridge platform – from where the submarine is controlled on the surface – was positioned by crane. As the building

Building sections (above left) and the special transporter.

Specialist techniques included (above) the profile grinding under temperature-controlled conditions of case-hardened materials for the main propulsion gearing, and (below) machining of the main gearbox using advanced stress analysis, to ensure uniform load distribution on the teeth and most importantly, minimum noise generation.

Hull frames and shell plates were built up on special formers (above) to form hoop-like units which were then milled for accurate edging. After being radiographed and tested, these small units were placed in large rolling machines for welding together into the big sub-assemblies (below). Specialist engineers from the quality control organizations of the companies involved, inspected and controlled all the production work in such vital areas as welding and glazing.

programme progressed there were yet more daily, weekly, monthly and bi-monthly meetings between the government experts and contractors, to monitor progress and ensure the work was on schedule. The *Resolution* was on the slipway for only 30 months from keel to launch, and during that time most of the machinery and equipment was installed, and a comprehensive test programme carried out. Finally, on 26 February 1964, Sir Alfred J. Sims, then Director General Ships (Bath) – where thousands of specialists were employed designing British warships – laid the keel of the submarine. The keel in this case being a 100-ton circular section of the pressure hull!

Meanwhile, supplies of the special steel were building up at Barrow for the construction of HMS *Repulse*, and Cammell Laird on Merseyside began 'bustling' into the nuclear age after a statement – reported on 9 May 1963 – that they were to build HMS *Renown* and HMS *Revenge*. A 'high-level' welding shop was constructed together with a 'clean' welding shop for high-grade welding of nuclear piping. A central clean store was added for storage and inspection of the nuclear core and nuclear-grade equipment. A new jetty was built to accommodate two huge cranes serving the submarines, and new administrative offices were built to house in one building all the contractor's representatives, naval personnel, test and installation engineers, and the builder's own staff of specialists. There was also a

HMS *Renown* nearing completion at Cammell Laird.

The vast shipbuilding complex at Barrow with HMS *Repulse* (centre foreground) in her berth, and below, the *Resolution* being built.

The size, girth and bulk of these huge submarines are truly apparent only at launch, when they tower 60 ft high. On 15 September 1966, HMS *Resolution* (left) was launched by HM The Queen Mother, and the then Chairman of Vickers (Major-General Sir Charles Dunphie) said: 'It is a great day for Barrow, a great day for Vickers and I believe, a great day for the Royal Navy.' Seen below is HMS *Renown* being launched by Mrs Healey, wife of Mr Denis W. Healey MP, MBE, the then Secretary of State for Defence, on 25 February 1967.

As Rear-Admiral Shepherd wrote: 'To achieve this goal within the specified time scale needed dedication probably unsurpassed in naval history.' Work on the submarines continued round the clock, as this fine night shot taken at the Barrow complex of Vickers shows. It meant that the *Resolution* was only on the slipway for 30 months from keel-laying to launch. Right is a Polaris submarine in her natural element for the first time.

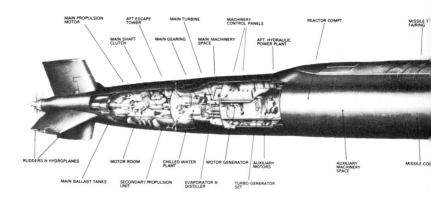

MAIN PROPULSION MOTOR · AFT ESCAPE TOWER · MAIN TURBINE · MACHINERY CONTROL PANELS · REACTOR COMPT. · MISSILE T FAIRING

MAIN SHAFT CLUTCH · MAIN GEARING · MAIN MACHINERY SPACE · MAIN MACHINERY · AFT. HYDRAULIC POWER PLANT

RUDDERS & HYDROPLANES · MOTOR ROOM · CHILLED WATER PLANT · MOTOR GENERATOR · AUXILIARY MOTORS · AUXILIARY MACHINERY SPACE · MISSILE CO

MAIN BALLAST TANKS · SECONDARY PROPULSION UNIT · EVAPORATOR & DISTILLER · TURBO-GENERATOR SET

'vat' room and cleaning department to provide facilities for acid-cleaning pipes and their assemblies, with an associated clean store for sealing cleaned parts for storage or dispatch.

It was a mammoth planning job to co-ordinate, monitor and progress chase – the biggest and most complex project ever undertaken by the yard. Finally, on 25 June 1964, the keel of the *Renown* was laid by Rear-Admiral (later Vice-Admiral Sir) Charles Piercy Mills, KCG CBE DSC (Director General Weapons (Navy)). With him on the platform were: Vice-Admiral Sir Hugh Mackenzie, Rear-Admiral I. J. Galantin, Officer-in-Charge of the USN Polaris programme, Mr G. Moss, then Director and General Manager of the Polaris Project in the shipyard (later Managing Director), and Mr R. W. Johnson, CBE, then Chairman of the company.

Polaris submarines are 425 ft long, have a beam of 33 ft and displace 7,500 ton surfaced and 8,400 ton submerged. With three deck levels, each with comfortable standing room, they have an underwater speed in excess of 25 knots. Right forward are the advanced sonar and the six 21-inch torpedo tubes capable of firing all the most modern underwater weapons.

The wireless room is fitted with very advanced equipment for the reception and transmission of data to other submarines, ships or aircraft in company, and messages can be received underwater.

These submarines are fitted with a wide variety of sensors and in the control room beneath the fin, their input – and that from other sources – can be processed and displayed to provide the Captain with a constantly updated picture of the tactical situation.

The Ships' Inertial Navigation Systems (SINS) are built by the

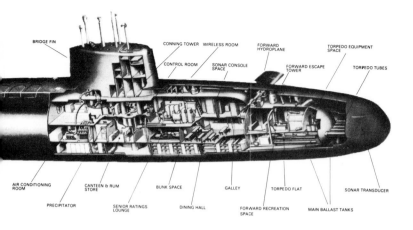

BRIDGE FIN · CONNING TOWER · WIRELESS ROOM · FORWARD HYDROPLANE · TORPEDO EQUIPMENT SPACE · CONTROL ROOM · SONAR CONSOLE SPACE · FORWARD ESCAPE TOWER · TORPEDO TUBES

AIR CONDITIONING ROOM · CANTEEN & RUM STORE · BUNK SPACE · GALLEY · TORPEDO FLAT · SONAR TRANSDUCER · PRECIPITATOR · SENIOR RATINGS LOUNGE · DINING HALL · FORWARD RECREATION SPACE · MAIN BALLAST TANKS

North American Aviation Company, and are similar to those fitted in American submarines. They are a combination of precision gyroscopes, accelerometers and computers, which measure and remember true North and the ship's heading, position and speed through the water, thus providing the extremely accurate data necessary for the successful launching of a missile.

The missile section virtually divides the submarine in two and houses the launching tubes in two rows of eight. Each missile has three warheads and a range of 2,880 miles.

Particular attention is given to ventilation, air-conditioning and waste disposal. A constant supply of pure air is provided by electrolysers which extract oxygen from sea-water. High-voltage precipitators keep dust out of the ship's atmosphere which is closely monitored throughout the ship for any radiation content. Other units remove carbon dioxide from the air.

Behind the missile section are the auxiliary machinery and reactor compartments. Steam-driven turbo-alternators and motors provide electrical supplies. Other systems include lubrication, steam, hydraulic, pneumatic and refrigeration.

HMS *Repulse*, third of the class, was launched on 4 November 1967 by Lady Joan Zuckerman, wife of Sir Solly Zuckerman, Chief Scientific Adviser to the Government.

HMS *Revenge* was launched from the Birkenhead yard of Cammell Laird on 15 March 1968, by Lady Law, wife of Vice-Admiral Sir Horace Law (later Admiral), KCB OBE DSC, then Controller of the Navy.

Each vessel has two crews of 144 officers and men. Known as the

Junior rates' dining hall and recreation space.

Port and Starboard Crews, they make maximum use of the submarines by taking turn and turn about on operational patrols, on completion of which, they return to the Clyde Submarine Base to change crews, restore and carry out maintenance.

Within the limits imposed by operational requirements, the crew's accommodation is designed to provide maximum comfort. In addition to their three-tier bunk spaces, junior rates have a recreation area and dining hall, while senior rates have a lounge, coffee bar and dining hall. A modern stainless-steel galley of which any housewife would be proud, has a number of labour-saving devices including an ice-cream making machine. It can provide meals for over 140 and a wide variety of hot and cold dishes. Specimen menu: soup, roast beef or curried

Officer's cabin and ward-room cold buffet.

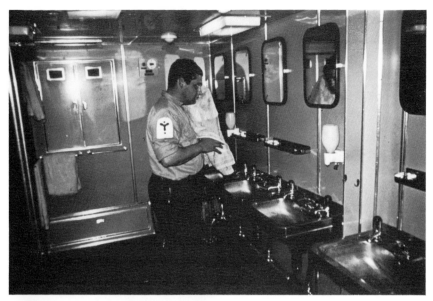

On any ship personal hygiene is very important and bathrooms, like the one above, are equipped to a very high standard with every modern convenience. Fresh water is supplied by two distilling plants each of which provides 5,000 gallons daily. This is enough for all machinery requirements and for almost unlimited domestic use, including the fine modern laundry seen left.

211

Captains R. J. P. Heath and J. B. L. Watson (below) – former Commanders of *Renown* and *Revenge*.

Above is Commander A. J. Whetstone (later Rear-Admiral, Flag Officer Sea Training and Chief of Naval Staff (operations) CB) and below, Commander J. R. Wadman (later Captain), both of HMS *Repulse*.

This shot of a typical commissioning ceremony gives some idea of the pomp
and circumstance of the most important moment in a ship's history.

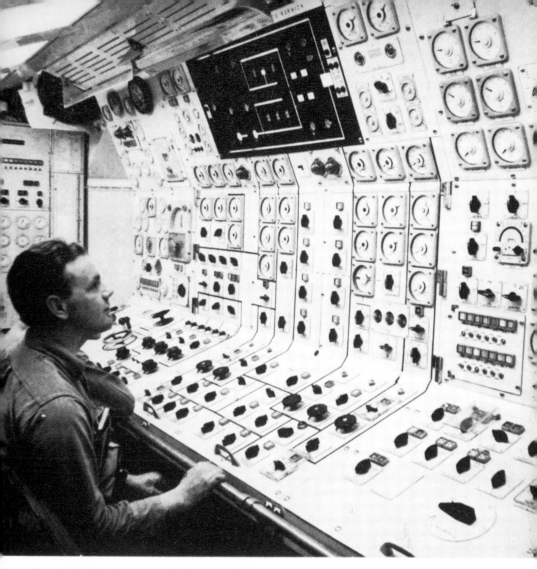

Not the inside of a space ship but one of the control panels in HM Submarine *Resolution*. Sophisticated electronics and high technology are, however, only as good as the men operating them and Submarine Command's training schools produce the highly trained and dedicated professionals needed to man the nuclear deterrent with complete safety.

chicken, ham salad, apple crumble or pineapple and cream, cheese, biscuits and coffee. There is an ample supply of fresh vegetables. Entertainment includes films, piped radio programmes, a library, daily news sheet and weekly magazine.

The *Resolution* is seen leaving the Barrow complex for sea trials off the north-west coast of Scotland, under the command of Commander M. C. Henry (Port Crew). For six weeks, the crew together with engineers from Vickers and various contractors, carried out an intensive programme of operational tests, including the high-speed test (below). The submarine later commissioned under Commander K. D. Frewer (Starboard Crew), joined the 10th Submarine Flotilla, and left for her first operational patrol.

The *Resolution* is shown with her hydroplanes out as they would be for submerged operations, and folded to reduce her beam on the surface.

HMS *Revenge* presents an unusual picture from astern.

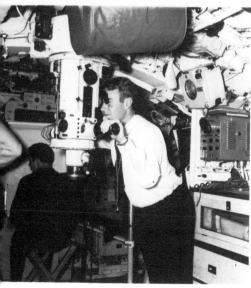

Two contrasting views of
different pattern periscopes as
fitted in British submarines.

219

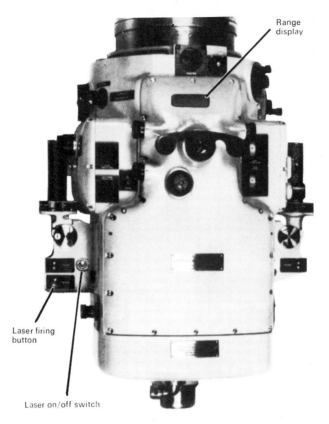

Range display

Laser firing button

Laser on/off switch

Today's periscopes are sophisticated multi-role instruments for day/night visual or electronic surveillance, fire control, and navigation. They have modern lenses giving a first-class image at differing magnifying powers for photography or electro-optical sensors. Masts have facilities for communications, radar, 'snort' induction and exhaust.

The modern data processing and computer equipment now fitted in modern submarines make it essential not only to have exact range figures for enemy attacks, but to have much better facilities available for watch-keeping through the periscope at night. To meet these needs, Barr and Stround have developed a laser rangefinder and an image intensifier to give very much improved night vision combined with accurate ranging. The laser rangefinder is fitted at the top of the periscope to ensure accuracy.

The laser rangefinder is instantaneous and accurate to within 32 ft over the whole spectrum. The controls consist of a main on/off switch

220

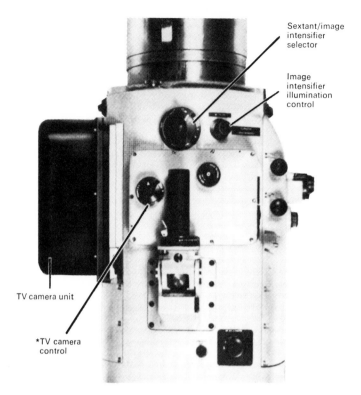

Sextant/image
intensifier
selector

Image
intensifier
illumination
control

TV camera unit

*TV camera
control

which is key-operated to avoid the eye hazards posed by laser beams and a fire button fires the laser on to the target. The range is projected into the eye-piece display. A range cut button wipes the display and allows another ranging operation to proceed.

The receiver consists of a photodiode that converts the reflected laser beam into an electrical signal which is then amplified by a sensitive low-noise circuit. High technology results in a 99.5 per cent certainty that it is a true target return and not a false alarm. A range logic board ensures electronic stop-watch accuracy to guarantee the accuracy of rangefinding.

The image intensifier uses a new design tube to produce a high level of amplification and can also deal with any bright lights which might be in the field of view. A large-aperture lens of 110 mm at the top of the main tube section focuses the maximum amount of light on to the photocathode of a TV camera unit. The resultant image on the tube's screen is projected via the main optical system designed for a six-times magnification. The system is accurately aligned with the laser rangefinder for use at night.

221

New Programmes

Although a report from the USN Research Laboratory indicated that the Americans were considering nuclear propulsion as far back as 1939, it was not until after the war that they began to consider making use of the US Army's Jupiter missile with its range of 1,728 miles. As it became obvious that the use of liquid propellants would pose unacceptable handling problems, a Special Projects Office was set up in November 1956 to manage the Fleet Ballistic Missile (FBM) programme. Prime contractors were the Lockheed Missile and Space Division and Aerojet General, who discussed with the Project Office the possibility of using solid propellants while keeping the Jupiter guidance and warhead.

General Electric developed the computer control system and the US Atomic Energy Commission broke through the weight/yield barrier with a dramatic reduction in the weight of the warhead. This brought the launch weight down to acceptable levels which made a submarine-launched weapon practicable.

On 8 December 1956, the name Polaris was given to the system and during 1957 the major contractors proceeded with the integrated system – a two-stage vehicle with multiple nozzles, jet deflection and a slender re-entry body. Rear-Admiral W. F. Raborn Jr who headed the Special Projects Office, drove the work on with unbounded enthusiasm. The missile emerged with an airframe of stainless-steel sheet, a rocket motor making use of a combustible fuel and inorganic, crystalline-type oxidizers.

The Sperry Gyroscope Company, working closely with the famous Massachusetts Institute of Technology (MIT) and the North American Aviation Company, developed the highly accurate inertial navigation system. The warhead had a 500 kiloton yield and the missile could be delivered with superb accuracy.

Each launch tube was isolated and shock energy was absorbed and dissipated by a complex damping system. The self-contained inertial guidance system in each missile was independent of external commands or control.

Today manufactured by the Lockheed Missile and Space Corporation, the Polaris A3 and their improved variants are two-stage ballistic missiles powered by solid-fuel rocket motors. They can be launched even when the submarine is surfaced and can hit the target with an accuracy measurable in yards. All the crew feel when a missile is fired is a hiss and slight shudder.

Armed with information from target computer tapes and the inertial

A Royal Navy Polaris missile breaks the surface after launch.

navigation system, the fire-control computers continuously calculate the flight instructions and pass them to the missiles, permanently ready in their tubes. Once launched, the flight path is controlled by the missile inertial guidance system which takes into account pre-firing data and in-flight behaviour.

At the front of the missile is the British-built and designed re-entry body containing the warheads, fuzing and arming devices, all in a special enclosure designed to withstand extremes of temperature when passing through the earth's atmosphere. When the system calculates that the warheads will reach the target in free-fall ballistic flight, the warheads separate from the second-stage motor and continue on to the target.

It will be appreciated by what has been said, that the navigation of a missile-armed submarine is of supreme importance. The exact position of the ship and target must be known right up to the moment of firing. The fire-control system itself makes use of 11 computers, and each missile carries one.

In 1972, the Commons Expenditure Committee concluded that the Polaris deterrent was adequate for the present. They were told that the 1972–3 support costs for Polaris were £39 m, excluding research and development, or 1.16 per cent of the Defence Budget. The cost of the four submarines was £162 m and that of the missiles £53 m.

There had never been a time without one submarine on patrol and studies suggested that there was an 81 per cent probability that at least one cluster of three warheads would penetrate the Moscow defences, and a 21 per cent probability that at least three more out of the 16 would do so.

There was a strong case for keeping the deterrent as it was but if Britain wanted to increase the range significantly, it would be better to wait for the Long Range Missile System (LRMS) rather than go for Poseidon, which would be an expensive luxury.

The committee estimated that by mid-1975, 31 out of the US Navy's 41 Polaris submarines would be fitted with 16 Poseidon missiles, able to launch 224 warheads of 50–60 kilotons each at 16 different targets within the space of 15 minutes. The cost of conversion was estimated at about £62–5 m for each submarine.

Equally, they were against building another Polaris submarine which would cost about £90 m including missiles and warheads, an expensive way of achieving a marginal improvement in capacity.

The committee was told that the Institute of Strategic Studies took the view that the submarines were extremely difficult to detect, and there was a great advantage in operating from the British continental shelf, under the protection of NATO, where A/S (anti-submarine) warfare was difficult.

The present submarines had a life of at least 20 years which meant that the oldest (*Resolution*) could remain in service until 1986, and the newest (*Revenge*) until 1990. The missile had a life span of only a few years but it was thought Britain had ample reserves.

Looking beyond Poseidon, the USN was researching two systems for an Under-sea Long-range Missile. ULMS-1 would have a range of some 4,500 miles and ULMS-2, 6,000 miles. The latter would need a new submarine and the two together were already being called the Trident system. Estimated cost with associated research and development was $1,350 m. The committee were by no means certain

FLEET BALLISTIC MISSILES

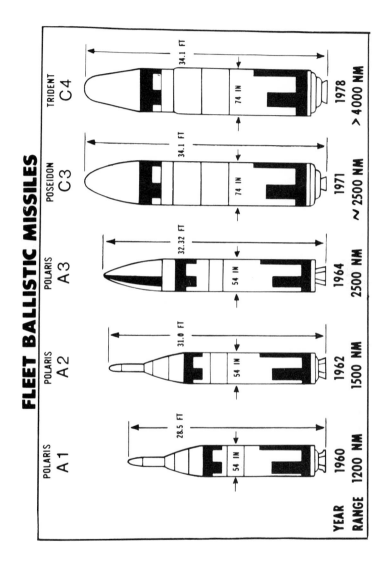

	POLARIS A1	POLARIS A2	POLARIS A3	POSEIDON C3	TRIDENT C4
	28.5 FT / 54 IN	31.0 FT / 54 IN	32.32 FT / 54 IN	34.1 FT / 74 IN	34.1 FT / 74 IN
YEAR	1960	1962	1964	1971	1978
RANGE	1200 NM	1500 NM	2500 NM	~ 2500 NM	> 4000 NM

A contrast in sizes showing (top left) a deck view of the *Ohio* during pre-commissioning activities with her missile tubes opened, and below it a similar view of a Polaris submarine.

The American Polaris programme ended on 2 June 1982 as the last of 16 A3 missiles was offloaded from the USS *Robert E. Lee* inside the explosive-handling wharf, US Submarine Base, Washington. The submarine (above) will be converted like others of the class to a nuclear fast-attack boat. The American Polaris era began in late 1955 when the Lockheed Corporation was given the order to build the world's first seaborne strategic missile. Lockhead had the missile ready by 1960, two years ahead of schedule. The first missile-armed submarine was the USS *George Washington*.

that the Trident would ever enter service but if it did, it was felt it would be too expensive for the UK.

In 1979 it was reported that Rosyth Dockyard were building a full-size section of a new submarine which it was hoped to introduce in late 1981 for explosive-shock and stress tests. It was said in the House of Commons in 1981, that this was the first they had heard of Chevaline and that the project and costs had been kept secret from the House for 10 years.

As in the case of the Government's decision to buy Trident, there was an immediate outcry from CND and dedicated left wingers. In fact, Chevaline had been developed by successive governments and was no great secret. Started by the Conservatives in 1970 and continued by the Wilson Government in 1974, it was an entirely British programme although there was full co-operation with the American Government on research, development and trials. In 1974, a research and development cost of some £240 m was approved for developing this new, sophisticated multiple warhead with decoys. The system combined all known penetration aids, making it virtually impossible for defences to prevent it getting through the outer ring. By 1976, costs were estimated at £450 m and in 1977, at £700 m. By then, the project was past the point of 'no return' and cutting it would have been a costly exercise because of contractual obligations.

On 24 January 1979, the then Defence Secretary, Mr Francis Pym, told the House that a £1,000 m programme – the estimated cost today – to give the four Polaris submarines an improved deterrent was nearly completed. Codenamed Polaris A3TK, Chevaline entered service with the Royal Navy in late 1982. BAJ Vickers was a major sub-contractor for this weapon system, the most complex development ever undertaken in the UK. Admiral Sir Henry Leach, then First Sea Lord said: 'Now that Chevaline has entered service with the Royal Navy, I send my congratulations to everyone who has played a part in the success of this vital and challenging project and my thanks for their hard work and dedication.'

On 15 July 1980, Mr Pym told the House that the Government intended to build a new fleet of four submarines armed with American Trident 1 missiles, each carrying eight British warheads of 50–60 kilotons.

The Trident submarines would be able to launch 128 nuclear warheads instead of the 48 of the Polaris Class, and with a range of 4,600 miles, the missiles would be able to hit any target in the Soviet Union.

The estimated cost was £5,000 m spread over the next 15 years.

Trident submarines would be a credible deterrent through to the 1990s. As with Polaris, the force would be British-owned and controlled, but committed to NATO – except in cases where supreme national interest was involved. During the next few years, said Mr Pym, the Government might order a fifth submarine at a cost of about £600 m.

In December 1980, Rear-Admiral John Grove (Chief Polaris Executive) told the Commons Defence Committee that British Polaris submarines were too good for the Russians. Arguing for the Trident deal, he said the Soviet Navy had never found patrolling Polaris submarines, but Soviet ones were invariably detected. This was possibly due to the Royal Navy having a 'very good sonar advantage over the Russians'.

Mr M. E. Quinlan, Deputy Under Secretary of State Policy and Programmes, pointed out that Trident was favoured over cruise missiles because of the invulnerability of the submarine platform, and the obvious economic advantages together with other benefits from further prolonged co-operation with the Americans. Trident would also give the submarines extra sea room in which to hide.

Sea room in which to hide! A vital aspect of this is speed. If a submarine travels at 10 knots and launches an attack which brings the A/S fleet to the area in 30 minutes, the submarine could be hiding anywhere within a circle of 104 square miles. At 20 knots the area increases to 416 square miles, but at 40 knots the area is 1,670 square miles – a lot of water to search in every direction.

In March 1981, however, the US Navy Secretary John Leahman said that if current production problems with the 18,000-ton lead ship of the Trident Class, the *Ohio*, continued, plans might have to be revised greatly. The Navy might be forced to turn to smaller submarines if the Electric Boat Company was unable to complete the submarine by the end of the year. The USS *Ohio* had been due for delivery in April 1979.

The trouble started in July 1977 when the Electric Boat Company told the Navy that there was a slippage of six months. The revised date for initial operational capability was August 1979.

Rear-Admiral Albert L. Kellin said in December 1977 that there had been a further six-month delay and the programme was revised forward to August 1980. On 18 June 1981, it was reported from Connecticut, USA, that the *Ohio* had begun sea trials, some 30 months late. In the meantime, the Navy had deployed the Trident misile in 10 of the 31-strong class of Lafayette submarines. These have 16 launchers instead of the 24 in the *Ohio*.

Four of the Ohio Class are now being built. So far named are the *Michigan* and *Georgia*. General Dynamics Electric Boat Division received the contract on 25 July 1974. General details released were: 16,600 ton on the surface; 18,700 ton dived; length 560 ft, beam 42 ft; 24 Trident 1 missiles, four 21-inch bow torpedo tubes; General Electric PWR with geared turbines producing 60,000 shp driving one propeller. Nuclear core life about 10 years; passive sonar only.

The modified Lafayette Class which formerly carried 16 Poseidon C3 missiles, displace 7,500 ton on the surface, and the first submarine was on patrol 31 March 1971. They displace 8,250 ton dived and were the biggest submarines then built in the West. With a beam of 33 ft and length of 425 ft, they had an underwater speed of over 30 knots.

A report in 1981 suggested that the latest Soviet submarines had been tracked at 40 knots and new ones might have a titanium body, giving a diving depth of 3,000 ft.

Submarines have traditionally relied on high-power, very low-frequency transmissions, on set frequencies at scheduled times, for the receipt of broadcast messages. Irrespective of whether or not the messages were of routine, operational or strategic importance, the submarine was not expected to even acknowledge receipt of the message in case the transmission gave away her position: this would put her two most important tactical assets of stealth and surprise at risk.

The advent of the nuclear-powered submarine able to range the world at high underwater speeds, has brought about a drastic change in command, control and communications, commonly known now as 'C³'. Central command and control is now of vital importance and there is a vast amount of sensor data which must reach the shore headquarters in time and reliably, if they are to exploit to the full the latest advances in underwater technology.

Any transmission from a submarine that is open to interception can give away its position and not only rob the force of stealth and surprise, but – with modern techniques – lead to the submarine's destruction. At the same time, the provision of secure, reliable communication links capable of withstanding an enemy attack, is of supreme importance.

So, key areas to be considered today are: the ability of submarines to feed back information of strategic importance so Command Shore HQ

Some idea of the enormous size of the Trident-armed submarines can be gathered from these contrasting views of the *Ohio* SSBN 726 (below) and the *Michigan* SSBN 727 (left), pictured during construction at the Electric Boat's yard. The vessels will be quieter, longer-ranged and independent of home bases. They represent a significant advance in technology – one of the main reasons for slippage in completion dates. Launch tubes are designed to accommodate new weapons as they become available.

The Trident-armed USS *John C. Calhoun*, a converted Lafayette Class Poseidon submarine casting off for the Demonstration and Shakedown Operation (DASO), during which the missile was launched. The support vessel USS *General Hoyt S. Vandenberg* (below) gets ready to leave harbour for the demonstration.

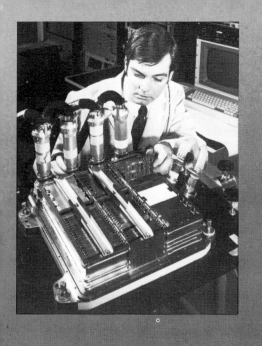

The 'shakedown operational launch of a Trident missile' off the east coast of Florida on 28 October 1980. Inset is the 'brain', one of the MK 5 electronic guidance assemblies built by the Hughes Aircraft Company, California. They are also one of the companies building the Mk 98 submarine fire-control system.

The unusual photograph (above) was taken from a USN Orion aircraft at a height of 20,000 ft and some 17 miles from the impact point of the re-entry body. It was a timed exposure of 40 seconds. The objects on the right are equipment sections burning up as they re-enter the earth's atmosphere, and the light flare at the base of each stream of light is reflection off the clouds.

This magnificent night-firing picture (left) was taken in July 1979 by a USAF photographer and supplied by the Naval Photographic Centre, Washington. It shows the 24th launch – the sixth submerged one – of a Trident missile, this time from the USS *Francis Scott Key*, at 22.12 EDT.

Seen left is another view showing the enormous size of the *Ohio*. Above is a section of the control room, and below an operator at the control console during a simulated missile firing.

can retain overall tactical control; the ability of the Shore HQ to pass information to the submarines; and the provision of secure, reliable communications links at all times and in all conditions.

The major part of the problem is how best to provide, through water or air, secure communications regardless of the submarine's speed, depth or position in the world. If a submarine must be near the surface to communicate effectively, this still places it at risk – a risk that cannot be accepted in this day and age.

Satellite communications, high-speed data links, short-burst transmissions on high power and even superimposing messages on Loran C (navigational frequencies) have all been considered. Another possibility is extremely low (16 HZ or below) high-power transmissions from dual sites, to increase the chances of surviving in the event of a nuclear attack.

In a fast moving, complex and 'deadly' future war, constantly revised information will be of vital importance, because it may be out of date in hours and tactical or operational advantages lost.

Although this immense, highly technical problem has not – as far as is known – been completely solved, there is no doubt that the expertise of British and American communication experts will find an answer to this problem in the near future.

For the submarine of course, there is another aspect of detection of supreme importance – propeller noise which can be picked up by surface or submerged enemy sensors. In the early days this was no easy problem to solve, by virtue of the fact that submarines used two different methods of propulsion, and operational needs demanded two different solutions.

High surface speeds were not compatible with high underwater speeds, because the resistance when submerged is greater. Propellers could be designed for one or the other purpose, but not both. With the advent of the nuclear-powered submarine able to remain submerged for months and completely self-supporting up to the limits of the food supply, propellers could be designed for the best submerged performance with vibration, cavitation, 'singing' and other noises, reduced to the lowest possible level. The submarine should now be able to operate over its entire speed range, at any depth, and hopefully undetectable from the surface – only time can tell if this target has been achieved, although the Navy has traditionally had a 'sonar advantage' over potential enemies.

RA Sir John Woodward, Flag Officer Submarines, who was Commander of the British Naval Task Force to the Falklands, photographed as a Commander in 1969 when Captain of HMS *Warspite*. He served in HMS *Maidstone* as a Midshipman and became a submarine specialist in 1954, serving in HMS *Sanguine* and HMS *Porpoise*.

In 1961 he commanded HMS *Tireless* and after taking the nuclear reactor course, HMS *Grampus*. He was then appointed as No. 1 of HMS *Valiant*. In 1976 he was Captain of HMS *Sheffield* and in 1978, Director of Naval Plans at the Ministry of Defence. Made Rear-Admiral in 1981, he took up the post of Flag Officer Submarines and the NATO post of Commander Submarines Eastern Atlantic in May 1983.

Admiral Sir John Fieldhouse, KCB, Commander-in-Chief Fleet, was made a Knight Grand Cross of the Order of the British Empire in the Falklands Honours List.

Shown here as Commander and Captain of the Royal Navy's first nuclear-powered submarine HMS *Dreadnought*, the Admiral was appointed as Chief of Naval Staff and First Sea Lord in December 1982.

The First Sea Lord qualified for entry into Submarine Command in 1948 and passed the Commanding Officer's Course in 1955, later commanding the *Acheron*, *Tiptoe* and *Walrus*. After completing the Nuclear Propulsion Course at RNC Greenwich and two years on the staff of Flag Officer Submarines (FOSM), he commanded the *Dreadnought* 1964–6. From 1968–70 he was Captain S/M 10 – the Polaris Squadron at Faslane – and as Commodore commanded the Standing Naval Force Atlantic. Appointed Deputy Director Naval Warfare (MOD) in February 1973, he was promoted to Rear-Admiral in 1974 and FOSM in November 1977. Honoured by the KCB in 1980, he was promoted to Admiral in 1981 and became C-in-C Fleet on 14 May 1981, with overall control of the Task Force at sea.

Appendix
Class Specifications

In the leading particulars, surfaced and submerged figures are given for weight displacements and speeds. These are measured in tons and knots respectively. Dimensions are in feet.

Following many enquiries, both at home and when on the Navy news desk, individual submarine details (name, completion date, and what happened to the submarine) are added for the historic classes up to 1927. Similar details for the later classes may be found in other standard reference books.

HOLLAND CLASS 1920–3

Displacement	*No. 1* 113/122
Dimensions	63.3 × 11.75
Torpedo Tubes	One 18-inch bow
Machinery	160-hp petrol engine
	70-hp electric motor
Speed	7.5/6
Crew	7
Built	Vickers

No. 1	1902	1913 sold, sank under tow off Plymouth. Raised 1982 for museum
No. 2	1902	1913 sold
No. 3	1903	1911 sunk in experiments
No. 4	1902	1912 dismantled
No. 5	1903	1912 sank on tow to breakers

A CLASS 1903–5

Displacement	*A1–4* 190/207 *A5–13* 190/205.5
Dimensions	*A2–13* 105.5 × 12.75
Torpedo Tubes	Two 18-inch
Machinery	*A1–4* 450-hp petrol engine, 80-hp electric motor
	A5–12 600-hp petrol engine, 150-hp electric motor
Speed	11.5/7
Crew	11–14
Built	Vickers

A1 was laid down as *Holland No. 6*. *A13* had a heavy-oil engine

241

A1	1903	1904 sunk, collision off Portsmouth
A2	1904	1920 wrecked, 1925 sold
A3	1904	1912 sunk, collision off I. of Wight
A4	1904	1905 sunk, collision off Portsmouth
A5	1904	1920 dismantled
A6	1904	1920 sold
A7	1905	1914 foundered off Plymouth
A8	1905	1920 sold
A9	1905	1920 scrapped
A10	1905	1919 sold
A11	1905	1920 scrapped
A12	1905	1920 sold
A13	1905	1920 scrapped

B CLASS 1905–6

Displacement	280/313
Dimensions	142 × 13.5
Torpedo Tubes	Two 18-inch
Machinery	600-hp petrol engine
	190-hp electric motor One screw
Speed	12/6
Crew	16
Built	Vickers

B1 was laid down as *A14*

B1	1905	1922 sold
B2	1905	1912 sunk, collision off Dover
B3	1906	1919 sold
B4	1906	1919 sold
B5	1906	1922 sold
B6	1906	1919 sold, scrapped in Italy
B7	1906	1919 sold, scrapped at Malta
B8	1906	1919 sold
B9	1906	1919 sold, scrapped in Italy
B10	1906	1916 bombed in dock at Venice
B11	1906	1919 sold, scrapped in Italy

C CLASS 1906–10

Displacement	290/320
Dimensions	143 × 13.5
Torpedo Tubes	Two 18-inch

242

Machinery		600-hp petrol engine
		300-hp electric motor One screw
Speed		13/7.5
Crew		16
Built		Chatham Dockyard, Vickers

C1	1906	1921 sold
C2	1906	1924 sold
C3	1907	1918 blown up at Zeebrugge Mole
C4	1907	1922 sold
C5	1906	1919 scrapped at Malta
C6	1907	1919 sold
C7	1907	1919 sold
C8	1907	1921 sold
C9	1907	1922 sold
C10	1907	1922 sold
C11	1907	1909 sunk, collision off Cromer
C12	1908	1920 scrapped
C13	1908	1920 sold
C14	1908	1921 sold
C15	1908	1922 sold
C16	1908	1922 sold
C17	1908	1919 sold
C18	1908	1921 sold
C19	1909	1920 sold
C20	1910	1921 sold
C21	1909	1921 sold
C22	1909	1920 sold
C23	1909	1921 sold
C24	1909	1921 sold
C25	1909	1921 sold
C26	1909	1918 blown up at Helsingfors
C27	1909	1918 blown up at Helsingfors
C28	1909	1921 sold
C29	1909	1915 mined in the North Sea
C30	1909	1921 sold
C31	1909	1915 lost off Belgian Coast
C32	1909	1917 stranded and blown up, Gulf of Riga
C33	1910	1915 lost in the North Sea
C34	1910	1917 sunk by *U52* off Shetland Islands
C35	1910	1918 blown up at Helsingfors
C36	1910	1919 scrapped in China
C37	1910	1919 scrapped in China
C38	1910	1919 scrapped in China

D CLASS 1910–12

Displacement	*D1* 483/595 *D2–8* 495/620
Dimensions	162 × 20.5
Torpedo Tubes	Three 18-inch; two bow, one stern
Guns	First small gun in *D4* *D2–8* one 12-pdr
Machinery	*D1* 1,200-hp diesel engine, 550-hp electric motor
	D2–8 750-hp diesel engine, 550-hp electric motor
	Twin screw
Speed	*D1* 14/10 *D2–8* 16/10
Crew	25
Built	Chatham Dockyard, Vickers

D1	1910	1918 sunk as target
D2	1911	1914 lost in the North Sea
D3	1911	1918 bombed (in error), by French airship
D4	1911	1921 sold
D5	1912	1914 mined off east coast
D6	1912	1918 sunk by U-boat off N. Ireland
D7	1911	1921 sold
D8	1912	1921 sold

E CLASS 1913–16

Displacement	660/800
Dimensions	181 × 22.5
Torpedo Tubes	Five 18-inch; two bow, two beam, one stern
Guns	One, various calibre
Machinery	1,600-hp diesel engine
	840-hp electric motor Twin screws
Speed	16/10
Crew	30
Built	Armstrong Whitworth, Cammell Laird, Chatham Dockyard, Denby, Devonport Dockyard, Fairfield/Beardmore, Swan Hunter, Thornycroft, Vickers, Yarrow

E1 and *2* were laid down as *D9* and *10*. Minelayers (ML) had no beam tubes but had mine tubes and carried 20 mines. *E28* was cancelled during the war

E1	1913	1918 blown up at Helsingfors
E2	1913	1921 sold at Malta
E3	1915	1914 torpedoed by *U27* off Borkum
E4	1913	1922 sold
E5	1913	1916 sunk by cruiser *Strassburg* in North Sea
E6	1913	1915 mined in North Sea

E7	1913	1915 sunk at the Dardanelles
E8	1913	1918 blown up at Helsingfors

R.A.N. ships

AE1	1914	1914 lost in Pacific (struck uncharted reef?)
AE2	1914	1915 sunk by Turkish warships in Sea of Marmara

E9 type

E9	1913	1918 blown up at Helsingfors
E10	1914	1915 lost in the North Sea
E11	1914	1921 sold at Malta
E12	1914	1921 sold at Malta
E13	1914	1915 stranded on Danish coast. 1921 sold
E14	1914	1918 sunk at the Dardanelles
E15	1914	1915 stranded at the Dardanelles and destroyed
E16	1915	1916 mined in Heligoland Bight
E17	1915	1916 wrecked off Texel
E18	1915	1916 mined in the Baltic
E19	1915	1918 blown up at Helsingfors
E20	1915	1915 torpedoed by *UB14* in Sea of Marmara

E21 type

E21	1915	1921 sold
E22	1915	1916 torpedoed by *UB18* in North Sea
E23	1915	1922 sold
E24 (ML)	1916	1916 mined in Heligoland Bight
E25	1915	1921 sold
E26	1915	1916 lost in North Sea
E27	1917	1922 sold
E29	1915	1922 sold
E30	1915	1916 lost in North Sea
E31	1915	1922 sold
E32	1916	1922 sold
E33	1916	1922 sold
E34 (ML)	1917	1918 mined in Heligoland Bight
E35	1916	1922 sold
E36	1916	1917 lost, collision in North Sea
E37	1916	1916 lost in North Sea
E38	1916	1922 sold
E39	1916	1921 sold
E40	1917	1921 sold
E41 (ML)	1916	1922 sold
E42	1916	1922 sold
E43	1916	1921 sold
E44	1916	1921 sold
E45 (ML)	1916	1922 sold
E46 (ML)	1916	1922 sold

E47	1916	1917 lost in North Sea
E48	1917	1921 target, 1928 sold
E49	1916	1917 mined off Shetland Islands
E50	1917	1918 mined in North Sea
E51 (ML)	1917	1921 sold
E52	1917	1921 sold
E53	1916	1922 sold
E54	1916	1921 sold
E55	1916	1922 sold
E56	1916	1923 sold

SCOTT-LAURENTI CLASS 1914–15

Displacement	265/386
Dimensions	148 × 14
Torpedo Tubes	Two 18-inch bow
Machinery	650-hp diesel engine
	400-hp electric motor Twin screws
Speed	13.5/8.5
Crew	18
Built	Scotts

S1	1914	
S2	1915	} Oct. 1915 sold to Italy
S3	1915	

ARMSTRONG-LAUBAUF CLASS 1915

Displacement	340/508
Dimensions	171.5 × 15.3
Torpedo Tubes	Two 18-inch bow
Machinery	710-hp diesel engine
	480-hp electric motor Twin screws
Speed	13/8.5
Crew	19
Built	Armstrong Whitworth

W1	1915	July 1916 sold to Italy

VICKERS SPECIAL CLASS 1915–16

Displacement	364/486
Dimensions	147.5 × 16.25

246

Torpedo Tubes		Two 18-inch bow
Machinery		900-hp diesel engine
		380-hp electric motor Twin screws
Speed		14/9
Crew		18
Built		Vickers

V1	1915	1921 sold
V2	1915	1921 sold
V3	1916	1920 sold
V4	1916	1920 sold

F CLASS 1915–17

Displacement		353/525
Dimensions		151.5 × 16
Torpedo Tubes		Three 18-inch; two bow, one stern
Guns		One 12-pdr
Machinery		900-hp diesel engine
		400-hp electric motor Twin screws
Speed		14.5/9
Crew		20
Built		Chatham Dockyard, Thornycroft, White
		F4–8 were cancelled

F1	1915	1920 sold
F2	1917	1922 sold
F3	1916	1920 sold

G CLASS 1915–17

Displacement		700/837
Dimensions		181 × 22.6
Torpedo Tubes		One 21-inch stern Four 18-inch; two bow, two beam
Guns		One 3-inch
Machinery		1,600-hp diesel engine
		840-hp electric motor Twin screws
Speed		14.5/10
Crew		31
Built		Armstrong Whitworth, Chatham Dockyard, Scotts, Vickers

G15 was cancelled

G1	1915	1920 sold, 1923 scrapped
G2	1916	1920 sold, 1923 scrapped
G3	1916	1920 sold
G4	1916	1928 sold
G5	1916	1922 sold
G6	1916	1921 sold
G7	1916	1918 lost in North Sea
G8	1916	1918 lost in North Sea
G9	1916	1917 sunk (in error) off Norway
G10	1916	1923 sold
G11	1916	1918 wrecked off Howick
G12	1916	1923 sold
G13	1916	1923 sold
G14	1917	1921 sold

H CLASS 1915–19

Displacement	*H1–20* 364/434 *H21–52* 440/500
Dimensions	*H1–20* 150.25 × 15.75 *H21–52* 171 × 15.75
Torpedo Tubes	*H1–20* four 18-inch *H21–52* four 21-inch bow tubes
Guns	One 12-pdr
Machinery	480-hp diesel engine
	320-hp electric motor Twin screws
Speed	11.5/10
Crew	22
Built	Armstrong Whitworth, Beardmore, Cammell Laird, Pembroke Dockyard, Vickers (Montreal), Fore River (USA)

H35–40 and *H46* were cancelled

H1	1915	1921 sold at Malta
H2	1915	1921 sold at Malta
H3	1915	1916 sunk in the Adriatic
H4	1915	1921 sold at Malta
H5	1915	1918 sunk, collision in Irish Sea
H6	1915	1916 stranded in Holland and became Dutch *O8*
H7	1915	1921 sold at Malta
H8	1915	1921 sold
H9	1915	1921 sold at Malta
H10	1915	1918 lost in North Sea
H11	1915	1921 sold
H12	1915	1921 sold
H13	1915	1917 became Chilean *H1*
H14	1915	1919 became R.C.N. *CH14*, 1925 scrapped
H15	1915	1919 became R.C.N. *CH15*, 1925 scrapped
H16	1915	1917 became Chilean *H2*

H17	1915	1917 became Chilean *H3*
H18	1915	1917 became Chilean *H4*
H19	1915	1917 became Chilean *H5*
H20	1915	1917 became Chilean *H6*

H21 type

H21	1918	1926 sold
H22	1918	1929 sold
H23	1918	1934 sold
H24	1918	1934 sold
H25	1918	1929 sold
H26	1918	1928 sold
H27	1919	1935 sold
H28	1918	1944 sold
H29	1918	1926 sank in Devonport Dockyard, 1927 sold
H30	1918	1935 sold
H31	1919	1941 lost off Brest
H32	1919	1944 scrapped
H33	1919	1944 scrapped
H34	1919	1945 scrapped
H41	1919	1920 sold after being damaged in dock
H42	1919	1922 sunk, collision off Gibraltar
H43	1919	1944 sold
H44	1920	1945 sold
H47	1919	1929 sunk, collision off Welsh coast
H48	1919	1935 sold
H49	1919	1940 sunk by German ships off Dutch coast
H50	1919	1945 scrapped
H51	1918	1924 sold
H52	1919	1927 sold

J CLASS 1916

Displacement	1,210/1,820
Dimensions	275.5 × 23
Torpedo Tubes	Six 18-inch; four bow, two beam
Guns	One or two 3-inch, 4-inch
Machinery	3,600-hp diesel engine
	1,400-hp electric motor Three screws
Speed	19.5/9.5
Crew	44
Built	Devonport, Pembroke and Portsmouth Dockyards

J1	1916	1919 to R.A.N., 1924 sold
J2	1916	1919 to R.A.N., 1924 sold
J3	1916	1919 to R.A.N., 1926 dismantled
J4	1916	1919 to R.A.N., 1924 sold
J5	1916	1919 to R.A.N., 1924 sold
J6	1916	1918 sunk (in error), in North Sea
J7	1917	1919 to R.A.N., 1929 sold

HMS SWORDFISH (S1) 1916

Displacement	932 1,105
Dimensions	231.25 × 23
Torpedo Tubes	Two 21-inch bow, four 18-inch beam
Guns	Two 3-inch
Machinery	3,750-hp geared turbines
	1,500-hp electric motor Twin screws
Speed	18/10
Crew	42
Built	Scotts

Swordfish (S1)   1916   1918 surface patrol vessel, 1922 sold

HMS NAUTILUS (N1) 1917

Displacement	1,441/2,026
Dimensions	242.5 × 26
Torpedo Tubes	Two 21-inch, four 18-inch beam, two 18-inch stern
Guns	One 12-pdr
Machinery	3,700-hp diesel engine
	1,000-hp electric motor Twin screws
Speed	17/10
Crew	42
Built	Vickers

Nautilus (N1)   1917   1918 battery charging vessel, 1922 sold

K CLASS 1917–23

Displacement	*K1–22* 1,980/2,565 *K26* 2,140/2,770
Dimensions	*K1–22* 330 × 26.6 *K26* 351.5 × 28

Torpedo Tubes	*K1–22* eight 18-inch; four bow, four beam
	K26 six 21-inch: four bow, four 18-inch beam
Guns	*K1–22* one or two 4-inch, one 3-inch AA
	K26 three 4-inch
Machinery	10,500-hp geared turbines
	800-hp diesel booster for diving or surfacing
	1,400-hp electric motor Twin screws
Speed	*K1–22* 25/9 *K26* 23.5/9
Crew	*K1–22* 50–60 *K26* 65
Built	Armstrong Whitworth, Beardmore, Devonport
	Dockyard, Fairfield, Pembroke Dockyard, Vickers

K17 was mounted with two 5.5-inch guns instead of 4-inch. *K23–5*, *K27* and *K28* were cancelled. In 1924, *K26* did a cruise to Colombo and back

K1	1917	1917 sunk, collision in the North Sea
K2	1917	1926 sold
K3	1916	1921 sold
K4	1917	1918 sunk, collision in the Firth of Forth
K5	1917	1921 foundered off Ushant
K6	1917	1926 sold
K7	1917	1921 sold
K8	1917	1923 sold
K9	1917	1926 sold
K10	1917	1921 sold
K11	1917	1921 sold
K12	1917	1926 sold
K13	1917	1917 foundered in the Gare Loch,
		raised to become *K22*
K14	1917	1926 sold
K15	1918	1924 sold
K16	1918	1924 sold
K17	1917	1918 sunk, collision in the Firth of Forth
K22 (see *K13* above)		1926 sold
K23 type		
K26	1923	1931 sold at Malta

L CLASS 1917–27

Displacement	*L1–8* 890/1,070 L9s 914/1,080 L50s 960/1,150
Dimensions	*L1–8* 231 × 23.5 L9s 238.5 × 23.5
	L50s 235 × 23.5
Torpedo Tubes	*L1–8* six 18-inch; four bow, two beam
	L9s four 21-inch bow, two 18-inch beam

Guns	L50s six 21-inch bow
	L1–33 one 3-inch or 4-inch
	L50s two 4-inch
Machinery	2,400-hp diesel engine
	1,600-hp electric motor Twin screws
Speed	17.5/10.5
Crew	*L1–33* 38 *L50s* 44
Built	Armstrong Whitworth, Cammell Laird, Chatham and
	Devonport Dockyards, Fairfield, Pembroke
	Dockyard, Sheerness, Vickers

L4 and *L17* later had their beam tubes removed. Minelayers carried 16 mines, in two vertical chutes of eight, each side amidships. *L28–31* and *L34–6* were cancelled. *L13* and *L37–49* were not ordered

L1	1917	1930 sold
L2	1917	1930 sold
L3	1918	1930 sold
L4	1918	1934 sold
L5	1918	1930 sold
L6	1918	1935 sold
L7	1917	1930 sold
L8	1918	1930 sold

L9 type

L9	1918	1923 foundered in typhoon at Hong Kong. Raised and sold
L10	1918	1918 sunk by German destroyer off Texel
L11 (ML)	1918	1932 sold
L12 (ML)	1918	1932 sold
L14 (ML)	1918	1934 sold
L15	1918	1932 sold
L16	1918	1934 sold
L17 (ML)	1918	1934 sold
L18	1919	1936 sold
L19	1919	1937 sold
L20	1919	1935 sold
L21	1920	1939 sold
L22	1921	1935 sold
L23	1924	1946 sold
L24	1920	1924 sunk, collision off Portland
L25 (ML)	1927	1935 sold
L26	1926	1946 sold
L27	1925	1947 sold
L32	—	1920 sold, uncompleted
L33	1924	1932 sold

L50 type

L52	1919	1935 sold and wrecked off Barry
L53	1924	1939 sold
L54	1924	1939 sold
L55	1918	1919 sunk in Baltic, 1928–31 salvaged by Russians
L56	1919	1938 sold
L67	1927	1927 sold to Yugoslavia
L68	1927	1927 sold to Yugoslavia
L69	1923	1939 sold
L70	—	1920 sold uncompleted
L71	1919	1938 sold

M CLASS 1918–20

Displacement	1,600/1,950
Dimensions	296–305 × 24.5
Torpedo Tubes	Four 18-inch or 21-inch bow
Guns	One 12-inch, one 3-inch
Machinery	2,400-hp diesel engine
	1,600-hp electric motor Twin screws
Speed	15.5/9.5
Crew	65
Built	Armstrong Whitworth, Vickers

M1	1918	1925 sunk, collision off Start Point
M2	1918	1927 altered to carry seaplane. 1932 foundered
M3	1920	1927 altered to ML. 1932 sold

R CLASS 1918–19

Displacement	410/500
Dimensions	163 × 15.75
Torpedo Tubes	Six 18-inch bow
Machinery	2,200-hp diesel engine
	1,200-hp electric motor One screw
Speed	9.5/15
Crew	22
Built	Armstrong Whitworth, Cammell Laird,
	Chatham Dockyard, Vickers

R5 and *R6* were cancelled

R1	1918	1923 sold
R2	1918	1923 sold
R3	1919	1923 sold
R4	1919	1934 sold
R7	1918	1923 sold
R8	1918	1923 sold
R9	1918	1923 sold
R10	1919	1929 sold
R11	1918	1923 sold
R12	1918	1923 sold

O CLASS 1926–8

Displacement	*Oberon* 1,598/1,831 *Oxley, Otway* 1,349/1,872
	Odin and rest 1,781/2,030
Dimensions	*Oberon* 270 × 28
	Oxley, Otway 275 × 27.75
	Odin and rest 283.5 × 28
Torpedo Tubes	Eight 21-inch; six bow, two stern
Guns	One 4-inch, two machine-guns
Machinery	*Oberon* 2,950-hp diesel engine
	Oxley, Otway 3,000-hp diesel engine
	Odin and rest 4,400-hp diesel engine
	1,350 electric motor Twin screws
Speed	*Oberon* 15/9 *Oxley, Otway* 15.5/9
	Odin and rest 17.5/9
Crew	50–4
Built	Beardmore, Chatham Dockyard, Vickers

P CLASS 1929–30

Displacement	1,760/2,040
Dimensions	289 × 28
Torpedo Tubes	Eight 21-inch; six bow, two stern
Guns	One 4-inch, two smaller ones
Machinery	4,600-hp diesel engine
	1350-hp electric motor Twin screws
Speed	17.5/9
Crew	50
Built	Cammell Laird, Chatham Dockyard, Vickers

R CLASS 1930–1

Displacement	1,763/2,030
Dimensions	287 × 30
Torpedo Tubes	Eight 21-inch; six bow, two stern
Guns	One 4-inch, two smaller ones
Machinery	4,600-hp diesel engine
	1,320-hp electric motor Twin screws
Speed	17.5/9
Crew	50
Built	Chatham Dockyard, Vickers

SWORDFISH CLASS 1932–3

Displacement	730/927
Dimensions	201 × 25
Torpedo Tubes	Six 21-inch
Guns	One 3-inch, two machine-guns
Machinery	1,550-hp diesel engine
	1,300-hp electric motor Twin screws
Speed	13.75/10
Crew	40
Built	Chatham Dockyard

THAMES CLASS 1932–5

Displacement	2,165/2,680
Dimensions	345 × 28
Torpedo Tubes	Six 21-inch
Guns	One 4-inch, two smaller ones
Machinery	10,000-hp diesel engine
	2,500-hp electric motor Twin screws
Speed	21.75/10
Crew	60
Built	Vickers

On trials *Thames* reached record speed of 22.5 knots at 405 revolutions, and apart from the Ks, was the first submarine to reach a speed of 21 knots. *Severn* and *Clyde* had slightly larger displacements

PORPOISE CLASS 1933–8

Displacement	1,786/2,050
Dimensions	289 × 29
Torpedo Tubes	Six 21-inch
Guns	One 4-inch, two machine-guns
Machinery	3,300-hp diesel engine
	1,630-hp electric motor Twin screws
Speed	16/8.75
Crew	55
Built	Chatham Dockyard, Scotts, Vickers

These were the only minelaying submarines then with the Royal Navy

SHARK CLASS 1934–7

Displacement	670/927
Dimensions	202.5 × 24
Torpedo Tubes	Six 21-inch
Guns	One 3-inch, two machine-guns
Machinery	1,550-hp diesel engine
	1,300-hp electric motor Twin screws
Speed	13.75/10
Crew	40
Built	Cammell Laird, Chatham Dockyard

UNITY CLASS 1941–4

Displacement	630/730
Dimensions	190 × 16
Torpedo Tubes	Four 21-inch bow
Machinery	615-hp diesel engine
	825-hp electric motor
Speed	11.25/10
Crew	31
Built	Vickers

S CLASS 1942–8

Displacement	872/1,000
Dimensions	217 × 23.75 × 10.5
Torpedo Tubes	Six 21-inch bow, one 21–inch stern
	13 torpedoes carried
Guns	One 3- or 4-inch
Machinery	1,900-hp diesel engine

	1,300-hp electric motor
Speed	14.5/10
Crew	48
Built	Cammell Laird, Chatham Dockyard, Scotts, Vickers

T CLASS 1942–6

Displacement	1,300/1,575
Dimensions	273.5 × 26.5
Torpedo Tubes	Eleven 21-inch when designed but when reconstructed seven 21-inch; six bow, one stern 17 torpedoes carried
Guns	One 4-inch, 3 machine-guns
Machinery	2,500-hp diesel engine 1,450-hp electric motor (later 2,900-hp)
Speed	15.25/9 (later 18 knots submerged)
Crew	61
Built	Cammell Laird, Chatham Dockyard, Devonport Dockyard, Portsmouth Dockyard, Scotts, Vickers

V CLASS 1943–5

Displacement	660/740
Dimensions	203.5 × 15.75 ×
Torpedo Tubes	Four 21-inch bow
Guns	One 3-inch, three 0.303 machine-guns
Machinery	3,300-hp diesel engine 1,630-hp electric motor
Speed	12.5/9
Crew	37
Built	Vickers

A CLASS 1945–8

Displacement	1,385/1,620
Dimensions	283 × 22.25
Torpedo Tubes	Six 21-inch; four bow, two stern 20 torpedoes or mines carried
Guns	One 4-inch, 3 machine-guns
Machinery	4,300-hp diesel engine 1,250-hp electric motor
Speed	19/8
Crew	60
Built	Cammell Laird, Chatham Dockyard, Scotts, Vickers

257

FAST EXPERIMENTAL CLASS 1956–8

Displacement	780/1,120
Dimensions	225.5 × 15.75
Unarmed	
Machinery	Diesel–electric
Speed	Over 25 knots submerged
Crew	49
Built	Vickers

PORPOISE CLASS 1958–61

Displacement	2,030/2,410
Dimensions	295.2 × 26.5
Torpedo Tubes	Eight 21 inch; 6 bow 2 stern 24 torpedoes carried
Machinery	Admiralty Standard Range diesels, two shafts, 3,680 shp
	Two electric motors, 6,000 shp
Speed	12/7
Crew	68
Built	Cammell Laird, Scotts, Vickers

OBERON CLASS 1960–7

The specifications are the same as for the Porpoise Class preceding. However, the Oberons were also built at Chatham Dockyard

DREADNOUGHT CLASS 1963

Displacement	3,500/4,000
Dimensions	265.8 × 32.2
Torpedo Tubes	Six 21-inch
Machinery	PWR
	Geared steam turbines, one shaft, 15,000 shp
	Emergency drive batteries and electric motor
Speed	25/30
Crew	88
Built	Vickers

VALIANT/CHURCHILL CLASS 1966–71

The two Valiant and three Churchill Class submarines have the same basic specifications

Displacement	4,200/4,770
Dimensions	285 × 33.2
Torpedo Tubes	Six 21-inch bow, 26 reloads
Machinery	PWR
	Geared steam turbines, 15,000 shp
	Emergency drive batteries and electric motor
Speed	25/30
Crew	103
Built	Cammell Laird, Vickers

RESOLUTION CLASS 1967–9

Displacement	7,500/8,400
Dimensions	425 × 33
Missiles	16 Polaris A3 with three 60 kiloton warheads
Torpedo Tubes	Six 21 inch bow tubes
Machinery	PWR
	Geared steam turbines, one shaft, 15,000 shp
	Emergency drive diesel generator, batteries and electric motor
Speed	25/30
Crew	143 (accommodation for 154)
Built	Cammell Laird, Vickers

The main turbo alternator is 1,700 kW

SWIFTSURE CLASS 1973–81

Displacement	3,500/4,500
Dimensions	272 × 32.3
Torpedo Tubes	Five 21-inch, 20 reloads
Machinery	PWR
	Geared steam turbines, one shaft, 15,000 shp
	4,000-hp auxiliary Paxman diesel engine
	Emergency drive batteries and electric motor
Speed	25/30
Crew	97
Built	Vickers

Bibliography

A Century of Shipbuilding, Tom Clarke, Dalesman Books, 1971.
A Damned Un-English Weapon, Edwyn Gray, Seeley Service & Co., 1971.
Brassey's Naval Annual (ten editions), RUSI, 1900–38.
Commissioning booklets on HMS *Renown, Revenge, Repulse, Resolution*.
Fear God and Dread Nought (three volumes), Arthur J. Marder, Jonathan Cape 1952–9.
Forlorn Hope, 1915, Admiral C. G. Brodie, W. J. Bryce Ltd, 1956.
HM Submarines, HMSO, 1945.
HM Submarines, Lt-Cdr P. Kemp, Herbert Jenkins, 1952.
Naval Memoirs, Admiral of The Fleet Sir Roger Keyes, Thornton Butterworth, 1934.
Naval Operations (Vol. 1), Sir Julian Corbett, Longman, Green & Co., 1920.
Red Star Rising at Sea, USNI, 1974.
Ships of The Royal Navy, Oscar Parkes, Gale & Polden, 1937.
Ships of The Royal Navy, Raymond Blackman, McDonald & Janes, 1973.
Straws in The Wind, Captain H. G. Stoker DSO, Herbert Jenkins Ltd, 1925.
Summary of British Warships, HMSO 1952.
The Battle of The Atlantic, HMSO, 1945.
The British Submarine, Cdr F. W. Lipscombe, Adam and Charles Black, 1954.
The Hunting Submarine, Ian Trenowden, William Kimber & Co., 1974.
The K Boats, Don Everitt, George C. Harrap & Co. Ltd, 1963.
The Royal Navy's First Submarine, Lt-Cdr J. M. Maber, Naval Historical Branch P.1001.
The Royal Navy, E. Keble Chatterton, Hutchinson & Co. Ltd, 1942.
Vickers Against The Odds 1956–1977, Sir Harold Evans, Hodder & Stoughton, 1978.
Warship International, No. 4 1979, The International Naval Research Organisation Inc., Ohio, USA.
We Dive at Dawn, Lt-Cdr Kenneth Edwards, Rich & Cowan Ltd, 1939.

Index

RN Polaris School, 164
Robeck, Rear-Admiral John de, 39
Roberts, Lt P. S., VC, 115
Robinson, William J., 15
Rolls-Royce Associates, 160
Roosevelt, President Theodore, 159
Ross-Turner, Vice-Admiral Sir Robert, 80
Rowe, Lt-Cdr C. A., 113
Royal Navy Tactical School, 81

St Vincent, Admiral Lord, 11
Sandford, Lt R. D., VC, 59, 62
Schofield, Lt, 62
Scott, Percy, 39
Scotts, 69
Selbourne, Lord, 14
Shepherd, Rear-Admiral C. W. H., 197,
  206
Sims, Sir Alfred J., 202
Slaughter, Lt-Cdr J. E., 106, 112
Smart, Lt J. E., RNVR, 123
Sperry Gyroscope Company, 222
Stevens, Cdr C., 80
Stoker, Lt-Cdr H. H. G. D., 53
Sturdy, Vice-Admiral Sir Doveton, 38
Submarines:
  A class, 21, 23, 40, 46
  Adder, 15
  Albacore, 159
  Alliance, 133
  Alpha Class, 154
  Andrew, 132
  Archimède, 68
  B Class, 21, 23, 39, 46, 51
  C Class, 24, 30, 39, 46, 62
  Conqueror, 66, 189
  D Class, 26, 39, 49
  Delta Class, 10
  Dreadnought, 164, 169–72
  E Class, 27, 33, 34, 37, 39, 41, 43, 46,
    48, 49, 53
  Excalibur, 154–8
  Explorer, 154–8
  F Class, 33
  G Class, 33, 34, 48
  H Class, 48, 64, 65, 108
  Holland Class, 9, 15, 20
  J Class, 68

K Class, 68
L Class, 65
M Class, 77
Nautilus, 11
Nautilus (N1), 33, 36, 68
Oberon Class, 134
O Class, 82
Ohio Class, 10, 229, 231
Orzel, 102
P Class, 66, 84
Plunger, 14
Polaris, 166–7, 199–211
Porpoise, 116
Porpoise Class, 134
R Class, 66, 84
S Class, 33
Seraph, 124
Shark Class, 85
Splendid, 119
Swordfish, 33, 34, 68
T Class, 86
Tally-Ho, 120, 121
Thames Class, 91
Trenchant, 123
Trident, 228–37
Type 2400, 146–50
Typhoon Class, USSR, 10
Unity Class, 93
V Class, 35
X Craft, 126
XE Craft, 123, 129, 131
Sutton, Cdr J. G., 80
Swan Hunter, 37

Talbot, Lt-Cdr, 43
Taylor, Lt, 58
Tennyson-d'Eyncourt, Sir Eustace, 68
Thorneycroft, Peter, 175
Thornycroft, 37
Tibbenham, Lt P., 174
Todd, Lt-Cdr Matthew, 97
Tomkinson, Cdr Wilfred, 31
Turner, Lt E. J. D., 125
Turner, Lt-Cdr R., 63

Varley, Cdr C. H., 64
Vickers, 15, 21, 24, 33, 36, 64, 68, 81,
  164, 197